# Getting Started with with Firebird

## Learning By Doing

Menkaura Abiola-Ellison

First published February 2019

Published by Fusion Enterprise Solutions (Holdings)
Communications House
290 Moston Lane
Manchester
M40 9WB

ISBN 13: 978-0-9932723-7-0

# About the Author

Menkaura Abiola-Ellison has over 33 years of experience as a software engineer and programmer.
He began his early years writing assembly code and BASIC in the 1980's, on his Acorn Atom that his parents purchased. He later went to university to study computer science, where he gained a BSc. Hon, and later an MBA in business.

For over 23 years he has programmed in various forms of Pascal from P-code, Module-2, Turbo Pascal, to Delphi/Lazarus, database application development.

In addition, he has commercial and technical experience in other RDBMSs such as MySQL/MariaDB, MS SQL Server, interbase and Firebird. However when it comes to deploying ISV or visualization environment, then Firebird comes up trumps.

The author has worked in medical electronics for 25 years, from ICU to Dental Systems Development, and has found that Pascal with a Firebird back-end to rise to all the challenges of the fast changing software world.

He felt that Firebird has been in the shadows for far too long, and believes that when considering a first database or more, that firebird is a great database to use.

In the many years he has worked as a software engineer, few database have stood the test of time as well as Firebird.

Menkaura has used Pascal database application, medical device management, embedded database applications, to name a few.

Menkaura is also the author of his previous book Getting Started with Lazarus and Free Pascal. It was through readers that enjoyed his previous book, requested that he write a similar book on Firebird.

# Acknowledgements

When writing a book it is not a one-man (or woman) operation, and therefore I would like to thank the people who helped take this from concept to reality.

Much of the material in this book attempts to address many of the questions I noticed being asked by many people coming to Firebird for the first time. Thanks goes out to those forums where people have helped others on their way to learning Firebird.

I would like to thank Lloyd Evering for the technical proof reading and many thanks to Adedotun Agbonin for painstaking testing the many code samples.

I am grateful to Dr Femi Biko for his constant support and encouragement.

Last but not least, a big thank you to my wife, Faith, for her support and patience.

My thanks to all those, not specifically mentioned by name, who contributed to this effort. You know who you are; and my apologies to anyone whom I may have inadvertently omitted. You have all demonstrated the spirit of what Firebird is about.

# Table of Contents

# Preface

### Why use Firebird?

When you think 'Firebird', a few adjectives come to mind, such as: extremely developer-friendly, powerful, multi-platform, multi-core, and truly Open-source, but these are just a few examples of this truly remarkable database. Firebird can hold its own when compared with such databases as MariaDB/MySQL, MS SQL Server, PostgreSQL, and more as we shall see in the course of this book.

### Firebird...

more reasons for choosing Firebird:

a/ It has a large and committed community.

b/ Used in schools, universities and the commercial world throughout the globe.

c/ Firebird can be installed on a wide range of platforms and devices.

d/ Large development tool support.

e/ Great for database application development.

f/ Easily scaleable from embedded to multi-user, multi-core.

### What this book covers

*Chapters 1 and 2,* introduce the reader to databases as a whole with a brief history and what lead to the relational database model along with the SQL language.

*Chapters 3 to 20,* introduce the reader to Firebird, and explains how to install firebird. In these chapters the reader will learn the fundamentals of Firebird, its Data Definition Language (DDL) and Firebird's Data Manipulation Language (DML). These chapters will further advance the reader's knowledge by introducing more advanced topics such as using Firebird's command tool isql, and introducing Dbeaver as a GUI for use with Firebird.

These chapters will expose the reader to core features of Firebird's SQL language.

*Chapter 21*, covers Full-Text-Search using a third party tool called Sphinx, and how it can be used with Firebird to perform very sophisticated and intelligent searches.

*Chapters 22 to 27*, delve further into the SQL language and look at such topics as Views, Store Procedures and Store Functions, Cursors, Triggers and Transaction processing. Globalization and localization is also covered.

*Chapters 28 to 30*, looks at managing security including access control, maintenance and general housekeeping, handling backups and recovery, garbage collection and the various tools that come shipped with every installation of Firebird.

*Chapters 31 to 33*, ends the book with a brief look at what we can expect in the up and coming version 4.0. The reader will take a fun look at LibreOffice Base and how Firebird can be used as a back-end to LibreOffice Base.

### What you need for this book

You will need to download the Firebird software that is supported by your computer operating system. (See chapter 3 on "Getting started with Firebird"). In addition, some of the examples presented in this book will require you to download third party components (such as Sphinx, discussed in chapter 21).

### Reader feedback

Feedback from readers is always welcome. Let us know what you think about this book, what you like or may have disliked.

To send us general feedback simply send an e-mail to *mka.feedback@gmail.com,* and mention the book title.

### Who is this book for?

This book assumes that the reader has no previous knowledge of Firebird, and may be new to computer databases altogether. This book is also intended for database application programmers who wish to migrate from another RDBMS such as MySQL/MariaDB, MS SQL

Server, H2, PostgreSQL, etc., and want to quickly get up to speed with Firebird.

This book is ideal for beginners and intermediates.

### Conventions

In this book, you will find a number of styles of text and icons that distinguish between different kinds of information. Below are the keys to the distinction:

(i) Really important points to remember.

`d` `i` `y` Things to try on your own –have a go!

# A word of warning

As this book is very much a hands on primer, the reader is expected to type the SQL script listed in the book. Therefore there will be NO code for you to download. The best way to learn SQL is by doing. The programs are intentionally included, the code included in the book is manageable enough to illustrate the necessary examples presented.

Half the fun is doing the work yourself, so have fun coding.

### Errata

Although I have taken every care to ensure the accuracy of its content, mistakes do happen. If you find a mistake in this book, I would be grateful if you would report this to me. By doing so, you can save other readers from frustration and help improve subsequent editions of this book. If you find errata, please report them to *mka.publishing@gmail.com*.

# 1 Introduction

On the 25<sup>th</sup> July 2000 Borland released the source code of it's Interbase Database. Within weeks of this release the Firebird project was born, and Firebird 1.0 was released that same year for Linux and Windows, Mac OS followed two years later.

Firebird is an open source SQL relational database management system (RDBMS) that runs on Linux, Microsoft Windows, Mac OS X and a variety of Unix versions.

One of the many great virtues of using Firebird is that there is a wide range of supporting programming languages that can directly access and manipulate the data. Languages include C, C++, Delphi/Free Pascal, Java, JavaScript, Node.js, Lua, Perl, PHP, Python and Ruby.

APIs and other access methods to the Firebird engine include: C/C++ API, OLE DB, ADO.NET, JDBC, ODBC. We will be looking at one or two in later chapters.

Firebird has matured over the years and is used by millions of people around the world.

In 2013 LibreOffice began the work of transitioning its embedded storage engine from HSQLDB to Firebird SQL backend. Firebird has been included in LibreOffice as an experimental option since LibreOffice 4.2. It is only fitting that we take a look at LibreOffice and Firebird with the aid of a simple application.

Even though Firebird has a very small footprint (minimal installation is 4Mb, standard is 33Mb), this small relational database management system performs excellently and scales impressively, from an embedded, single-user model to enterprise-wide deployments with multiple 2Tb databases running with hundreds of simultaneous clients. What more can be asked of her? Well that's what we will be finding out as we proceed.

Before we delve right in to the Firebird Relational Database Management System (RDBMS) let us look at some of the basics. If you are new to relational database management systems, this may seem daunting at first. Although the full scope of a database model's management, normalization etc; is beyond the scope of this book, the reader will benefit from a brief overview of some of the basics, which will aid the learning process.

### *The basics.*
Whether we are aware of it or not, we use databases everyday, whether to conduct an internet search, signing in to pick up our email or using an ATM to withdraw money – these services are all driven by database architecture.

### So our question is, "What is a database?"
The term 'database' (DB for short) means different things to different people. For our purposes we will use the term to mean a collection of data stored in some organized way. One way we may look at a database is to consider it as a filing cabinet. The filing cabinet is simply a physical location for storing data, regardless of what the data is or how it is organized.

### *So what is meant by the term Relational DBMS?*

To answer that, we need to take a quick peek into the past, (*just a tiny peek mind you*).
From the 1960s to the 1980s there were basically three common database models in use during that time.

These are:

   a) Hierarchical database model.
   b) Network model.
   c) Relational model.

### *Hierarchical database model...*
   The structure was developed by IBM in the 1960s, and used in early mainframe DBMSs.

   The hierarchical database model structures data as a tree of records, with each record having one parent record and many children. For example:

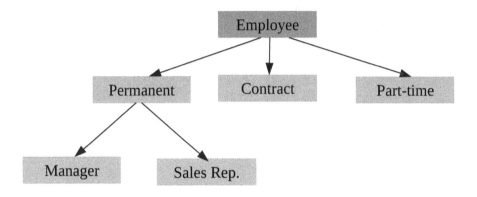

In the earlier days when data was stored on linear tape this DB model was ideal. The model relates very well to natural hierarchies such as assembly plants and employee organization in corporations.

Data at the top of the tree can be accessed very quickly.

However, as the data storage needs became more complex. Along with more sophisticated storage media, it became clear that another model is needed. One of the many disadvantages of using the hierarchical model is that the database can be very slow when searching for information on the lower entities. Another main issue with the model is it can only model 'one-to-many' relationships, and the more complex 'many-to-many' relationships are not supported. It also requires data to be repetitively stored in many different entities, which is wasteful duplication.

This led to the birth of the network database model.

### Network database model...

The network database model was designed to address some of the problems of the hierarchical model, particularly the lack of flexibility. Instead of only allowing each 'child' to have one 'parent', this model allowed each 'child' to have 'multiple parents'. The network models was originally invented by Charles Bachman and it's standard specification was published in 1969, however it was not until the 1971 second specification publication that most implementations were based on.

Example of a typical Bachman network model.

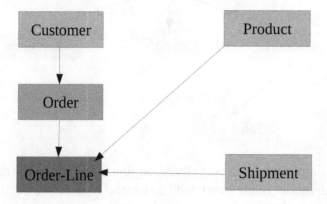

However although this model did address the inflexibility of the hierarchical model it also had problems why it is not used today. A picture paints a thousand words, so let's look at another network data model (schema) of a typical university.

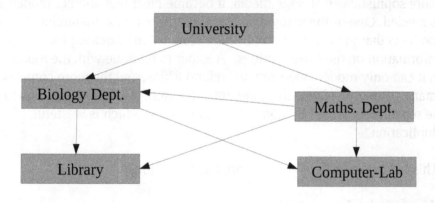

From the example diagram above you can see the complexity of the model. All the records are maintained using pointers and hence the whole database structure becomes very complex.

As a result insertion, deletion and updating operations of any record requires large number of pointers' adjustments. This makes the model more difficult to implement and maintain.

Although this model was more flexible than the hierarchical model, it still had flexibility issues, not all relations can be satisfied by assigning another owner.

Database practitioners were in search for a better database model. One that was flexible in design and simple to implement and maintain.

This gave birth to the Relational Database model (RDBM).

### Relational Database model...

The relational database model was such a success that it is still used today by tens of millions around the world. Instead of relying on a 'parent-child' or 'owner-member' relationship, the relational model allows any file to be related to any other by means of a common field. This resulted in a great reduction in complexity of the design.

The success of the relational database model goes to professor E.F. Codd who developed the model in 1970, however it was not until the 1980s that it began to become mainstream. A structured data manipulation language, for manipulating the data stored in this structure, was developed at the same time, known as Structured Query Language (SQL).

Consider the following example

Student Table

| Code | Name | Age |
|------|------|-----|
| SK765 | John Smith | 19 |
| FL065 | Fiona Jones | 20 |

Key

Course/Student Table

| id | Course_Code | Course_Student | Subject | Location |
|----|-------------|----------------|---------|----------|
| 1 | B25 | FL065 | Biology 101 | Block 103 |
| 2 | CO52 | SK765 | Computer Science | Computer Lab 2 |

A relational database is a set of tables containing data grouped into predefined data types. The relationship between them are simply expressed in terms of a simple set of keys. More on that later.

17

One great advantage of this model is that it is easily extendable to meet future required needs without requiring that all existing applications be modified, this saves database designers both time and money.

Another great advantage of the relational database model is the simplicity of the SQL language used to manipulate that data, where even a beginner - in a short period of time can learn to perform basic queries (a way of asking different questions about the data in the database and then getting the results back). This is a large part of the reason for the popularity of the model.

This leads us quite nicely into the Firebird implementation of the relational database and the SQL language.

### Put simply...

A relational database comprises of Tables, Columns and Datatypes, Rows, Primary Keys, Foreign Keys and the SQL language to manipulate the data. All these terms are explained below:

### Tables...

Tables are used to group (store) related data in a collection, the content will be specific to the DBMS software and may or may not be easily accessed by third party software without interface software (driver).

### Columns and Datatypes...

The columns within a table contain particular pieces of information, therefore each column in the table must be associated with a datatype. For example, if a field (column) is to store the order quantity then the data-type would be a numeric datatype.

*"What do we mean by the term datatype?"*
A type of *allowed* (or permissible, valid) data. Every table column has an associated datatype that restricts (or allows) specific data to be held in that column, for example a number column will allow numbers and numbers only to be stored in that column.

18

### Rows...

Data in a table is stored in rows and each record saved is stored in its own row. We first came across this in our Student and Course/student tables example above.

### Primary Keys...

Every row in a table must have a column (or set of columns) that *uniquely identifies it*.

(i) This is a fundamental DBMS concept. In the above example we gave each record an id field and each row had an incremental count, for each new data entered in our Course/student table.

### Foreign Key...

A Foreign Key is a key used to link two tables together. A Foreign Key is a field (or collection of fields) in one table that refers to the Primary Key in another table. We also first came across this in our Student and Course/student tables example above.

### The SQL language...

One of the main advantages of SQL is that it is not a proprietary language. Many DBMS support the standard SQL specification, however most DBMS suppliers also have a few non-standard features Firebird included.

(i) It should be noted that there is a standards committee that tries to define SQL syntax that can be used by all DBMS. In reality, no two DBMS's implement SQL identically. Therefore the SQL that will be discussed in this book will be specific to Firebird, and while much of the language discussed here will be usable with other DBMS's, please do not assume complete SQL syntax portability.

### What is SQL?...

SQL (Structured Query Language) is a language specifically designed to communicate with databases.

SQL is deliberately designed to contain few words. It is designed to do one thing and do it well – provide a simple and efficient way to read and write data from a database.

Advantages of SQL:

- SQL is not a proprietary language used by specific database vendors. Almost every major DBMS (Database Management Systems) support SQL, so learning this one language enables you to interact with just about every SQL type database you come across.

- SQL is easy to learn. The statements are all made up of descriptive English words, and there are not that many of them.

- Despite its apparent simplicity, SQL is actually a powerful language, and by cleverly using the language elements you can perform complex and sophisticated database operations.

# 2   Introduction to the Firebird Relational Database Management System (RDBMS)

This book is based on Firebird 3.0/4.0. As explained in the introduction Firebird servers come in two flavours, called *architectures*: Classic Server and Superserver.

As this book is aimed at the beginner and intermediates, we will be configuring Firebird server as a local connection.

Classic and SuperClassic offer an "embedded" local connection mode on Linux which is very fast, but not as secure as a regular network connection. On Windows, a separate Embedded Server is available which is even less secure, but can be very practical if you want to ship Firebird with your applications.

### Why Use Firebird...

Some of the key benefits why you would use Firebird are:

- Free to use both privately and commercially
- Fully featured SQL database engine
- Easily scalable from single user to enterprise-wide
- Fully open-source
- High functionality
- Compact small foot-print approximately 2MB

These are by no means the only benefits it has to offer, as you will discover as we journey through the book. So buckle up and let's get started.

### Installing Firebird

**Windows**
To install Firebird on Windows pc visit: *https://www.firebirdsql.org/en/server-packages/*
**and download the latest series. We will be using version 3.0 (a stable release).**

Click on the .exe file for your Windows operating system (OS).

Once downloaded, click the downloaded program and follow the installation instructions.

When you come to the screen below, Select options as shown below:

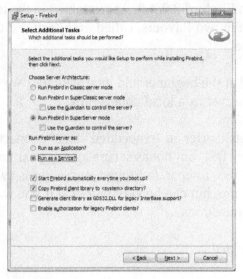

Click the next button, Leave the password fields blank. This will default the password to *masterkey.* Click the next button, then click the install button. Click the finish button when done.

### Linux

Firebird can be installed on a number of Linux Distros. The Linux distro used in this book will be elementary OS Loki. Elementary OS is based on ubuntu 16.x

To get the most up todate instructions visit: *https://firebirdsql.org/en/firebird-3-0/* for later version.

(i) *Note as of 2nd August 2018 Firebird 4.0 alpha (unstable version) is available from here:*
*https://www.firebirdsql.org/en/firebird-4-0-0-alpha1/*

You have now installed Firebird successfully.

Before we continue, I'll briefly discuss Client-server software and database management tools.

DBMS's fall into two categories: ***shared-file based*** and ***client-server based***. In the previous chapter I mentioned that LibreOffice has incorporated Firebird into its database office suite. However the LibreOffice default DBMS is called HQLDB. These types of databases are intended for single-user desktop applications and are referred to as shared-file based. Other similar shared-filebased applications include Microsoft Access and File Maker.

DBMS such as MariaDB, MySQL, PostgreSQL, Firebird, Oracle and Microsoft SQL Server are all client-server based databases. Client-server applications are split into two distinct parts:- server and client.

The ***server*** side software is responsible for all data access and manipulation. This software runs on the computer called a ***database server***. Only the server software interacts with the data files.

All requests for data operations from the outside world is funnelled through the server software.

The ***client*** software is the software that the user interacts with for making requests to the server. This software can reside on multiple computers from multiple locations.

## *DBMS's Tools...*

As mentioned above any client-server DBMSs requires client software to interact with it.

For Firebird there are many client tools available. When learning Firebird and any DBMS it is best to start with the tools provided by the makers of the DBMS.

However there are a few that are worthy of mention. These are:

- DBeaver that runs on all platforms that support the Java Virtual Machine (JVM);
- SQL Workbench available on Windows, Mac, Linux, and Unix based OSs;
- FlameRobin available on Windows, Mac, Linux, and Unix based OSs;

- LibreOffice Base available on Windows, Mac, Linux, Android (viewer for now), and Unix based OSs.

A full list can be found at: https://www.firebirdsql.org/en/third-party-tools/

But for now let us consider the command line tool that comes with Firebird.

### Firebird Command Line...

Every Firebird installation comes with a simple command line utility called: *isql*
similar to our command prompt for Windows or UNIX console.

### Using the command line utility...
### Windows...

Before you can use the tool, you may need to set the path to where Firebird was installed.

We can do this in one of two ways. You can launch your operating system command prompt and type the following SET PATH=%PATH%;C:\Program Files\Firebird\Firebird_x_x then click enter.

Alternatively, to make a permanent installation, you can edit your system environment. (Don't panic! It's quite straightforward).

**Step 1.1**
Do the following:

Click the start menu, then *right-mouse click on the computer icon*, select the properties option. Click on the *Advanced* tab (or *Advanced system* settings for Windows 7 and above), as shown below.

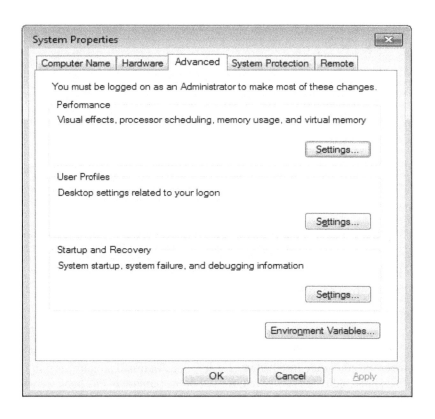

Now click the *Environment Variables* button. Under the *system variable* section scroll down and locate the PATH variable. Click on it to select it.

Now click the *'Edit...'* button, this will bring up a dialog box allowing you to add text to the end of your path for the *fpc* location. Press the End key on the keyboard and add the following instruction to the end of the text in the box as follows: *;C:\Program Files\Firebird\ Firebird_3_0* then click the *'OK'* button. Click *OK* on the rest of the Windows to close. Close all other system Windows. The location for Firebird is now permanently added to the system environment.

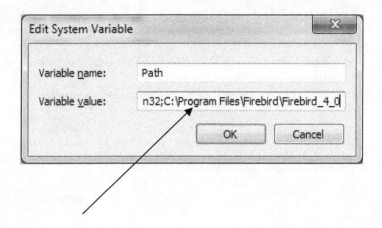

Please note the (;) semi-column at the beginning.
This tells the system this is the start of a new path location.

ⓘ Please note adding the Firebird path is not recommended, as this will override any future installed version location. To install a future version then either edit the entry or remove it. For the purpose of this book we will keep it set.

The *C:\Program Files\Firebird\Firebird_x_x* path may be different if you changed the installation path. Therefore locate the path and edit accordingly.

### Linux and Mac...

The installation would make the command line available.

Once you have set-up the path you are now ready to use the Firebird utility.

From your operating system (OS) prompt type *isql.* If you have installed it correctly you should see a similar screen as the one shown below.

```
C:\Users\dev2pc>isql
Use CONNECT or CREATE DATABASE to specify a database
SQL> _
```

For now, type: *exit; or quit;* and then press the *enter-key* at the Firebird prompt. This will exit you out of the Firebird utility and put you back to the OS command line prompt.

(i) exit; - will exit and commit changes

quit; - will exit and roll back changes

help; - will display a list and explanation of all the isql commands you can use.

```
C:\Users\dev2pc>isql
Use CONNECT or CREATE DATABASE to specify a database
SQL> quit;

C:\Users\dev2pc>isql
Use CONNECT or CREATE DATABASE to specify a database
SQL> exit;

C:\Users\dev2pc>
```

```
SQL> help;
Frontend commands:
BLOBDUMP  <blobid> <file>     -- dump BLOB to a file
BLOBVIEW  <blobid>            -- view BLOB in text editor
EDIT      [<filename>]        -- edit SQL script file and execute
EDIT                         -- edit current command buffer and execute
HELP                         -- display this menu
INput     <filename>         -- take input from the named SQL file
OUTput    [<filename>]       -- write output to named file
OUTput                       -- return output to stdout
SET       <option>           -- (Use HELP SET for complete list)
SHELL     <command>          -- execute Operating System command in sub-shell
SHOW      <object> [<name>]  -- display system information
     <object> = CHECK, COLLATION, DATABASE, DOMAIN, EXCEPTION, FILTER, FUNCTION,
          GENERATOR, GRANT, INDEX, PACKAGE, PROCEDURE, ROLE, SQL DIALECT,
          SYSTEM, TABLE, TRIGGER, VERSION, USERS, VIEW
EXIT                         -- exit and commit changes
QUIT                         -- exit and roll back changes

All commands may be abbreviated to letters in CAPitals
SQL>
```

*Working with Firebird...*

Create a workspace folder for example *'c:\myapp\data'*

Let us begin by creating a database. From within the *isql* tool type the following:

```
CREATE DATABASE 'C:\myapp\data\myapp.fdb' page_size
```
8192 *then press enter-key*

Now type:

```
user SYSDBA password 'masterkey';
```
*then press enter-key.*

This will create the file 'myapp.fdb' in the 'C:\myapp\data' folder.

Note SYSDBA is the default system admin username and 'masterkey' the password.

Now type quit; to *exit;* the isql utility.  Now whenever you wish to connect to your database simply do

As shown below.

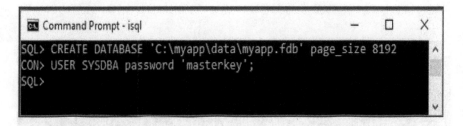

(i) Note the first line ending **without** (;)
placing (;) at the end of statement tell Firebird this is the end of the statement and to execute the statement.

(i)  A word of warning: it is never a good idea to log-in to Firebird as System Administrator when doing day-to-day querying.  However, in this particular case (as this is a new installation) there is no other user set up.

Now, to verify that we are connected to our database type the following:

```
SELECT * FROM RDB$RELATIONS;
```
*then press enter-key*

At this point the screen will be filled as follows:

```
     <null> DEU2PC                              SQL$DEFAULT19      6:1e0
11>                 0                                                        <nu
RDB$RUNTIME:
BLOB display set to subtype 1. This BLOB: subtype = 5
===================================================================================
         <null>              <null>              <null>              19
  1                  0              0         4 RDB$TRANSACTIONS                 S
QL$383                         <null>
                                                 <null>
     <null> DEU2PC                              SQL$DEFAULT20                <nu
11>                 0
     RDB$VIEW_BLR      RDB$VIEW_SOURCE    RDB$DESCRIPTION RDB$RELATION_ID RDB$SYSTEM
FLAG RDB$DBKEY_LENGTH RDB$FORMAT RDB$FIELD_ID RDB$RELATION_NAME          R
DB$SECURITY_CLASS                RDB$EXTERNAL_FILE
                                        RDB$RUNTIME RDB$EXTERNAL_DE
SCRIPTION RDB$OWNER_NAME                    RDB$DEFAULT_CLASS               RDB$FL
GS RDB$RELATION_TYPE
===================================================================================
===================================================================================
===================================================================================
         <null>              <null>              <null>              20
  1                  0              0         8 RDB$GENERATORS                   S
QL$384                         <null>
```

You can view useful information about your database by typing the following:

show DATABASE myapp.fdb; *then press enter-key*

```
SQL> show DATABASE myapp.fdb;
Database: c:\myapp\data\myapp.fdb
        Owner: DEU2PC
PAGE_SIZE 8192
Number of DB pages allocated = 180
Number of DB pages used = 176
Number of DB pages free = 4
Sweep interval = 20000
Forced Writes are ON
Transaction - oldest = 3
Transaction - oldest active = 11
Transaction - oldest snapshot = 11
Transaction - Next = 16
ODS = 12.0
Database not encrypted
Default Character set: NONE
SQL>
```

Now let us create a user *staff* with firstname *staffmember* and password *mypass* and grant administrators privileges. Type the following:

CREATE USER staff PASSWORD 'mypass' FIRSTNAME
'staffmember' GRANT ADMIN ROLE; *then press enter-key.*

This will add the user staff to the Firebird. We can check this by typing the following:

show users;

29

ⓘ   Note if you receive an access violation error as a windows user then this is usually a UAC access level issue. A quick solution would be to run isql as administrator user.

Note also if you receive the following message: *"Statement failed, SQLSTATE = 23000"* then locate the security3.fdb usually in c:\program file and give it full access for users "everyone" and "user" (windows pc)

## Congratulations! You have now setup your first Firebird database.

# Summing up chapters 1 and 2

## *Introduction*

In this chapter we took a brief look at the genesis of the Firebird project and how it came about, highlighting the various platforms that Firebird supports, along with supporting interface programming languages and APIs. In this chapter we also discussed other database models along with the relational database model.

We also took a closer look at the relational database model and the SQL language that is the specified language designed for relational databases.

We ended this chapter by briefly stating that a relational database comprises of Tables, Columns and Datatypes, Rows, Primary Keys, Foreign Keys and the SQL language to manipulate the data.

## *Introduction to the Firebird Relational Database Management System (RDBMS)*

In this chapter we introduced Firebird and installed Firebird on to your PC (Windows or Linux) and configured the environment.

We also introduced the command-line utility tool that comes with the installation and performed some basic querying. We rounded off this chapter be creating a database and setting up a user with admin privileges.

In the following chapters we will begin our exploration of Firebird and use its SQL language to create and manipulate the database.

# 3   Getting Started with Firebird

We ended the previous chapter by creating a database named *myapp* located in folder *c:\myapp\data* and creating a user, *staff*.

ⓘ If you are using Linux then insert the folder created in the previous chapter.

### *Connecting to the database*

Let us start by connecting to the database we created in the previous chapter. Start your terminal console or command prompt window (for window users).

Run isql

and type the following:

```
connect c:\myapp\data\myapp.fdb user SYSDBA
password masterkey;
```

> ### *then hit return*
>
> Note that this time connect string and user/password in one complete string

```
SQL> connect c:\myapp\data\myapp.fdb user SYSDBA password masterkey;
Database: c:\myapp\data\myapp.fdb, User: SYSDBA
```

By connecting to the database with user SYSDBA allows user SYSDBA to have automatic rights to anything within an individual database.

By connecting to our database we can now interrogate and manipulate the database.

### *Tables and the Database.*

When we connect to the Firebird database it may be handy to get a list of the tables it contains. We can do this be typing the following:

```
SHOW TABLES; then hit return
```

If this is a newly created database then you will get the following
return message:

```
There are no tables in this database
```

In the previous chapter we stated that Tables comprise of Columns and
Datatypes, Rows, Primary Keys, Foreign Keys and that the columns
within a table contain particular pieces of information, therefore each
column in the table must be associated with a datatype. For example if
a field (column) is to store the order quantity then the data-type would
be a numeric datatype and what we mean by that is that a type of
*allowed* (or permissible, valid) data. Every table column has an
associated datatype that restricts (or allows) specific data to be held in
that column, for example a numbers column will allow numbers and
numbers only to be stored in that column.

So let us now create our simple student table from the chapter 1
example.

Recap:

Student table

| Code | Name | Age |
|------|------|-----|
| SK765 | John Smith | 19 |
| FL065 | Fiona Jones | 20 |

### Create Table

Type the following:

```
create table student (
      code varchar(20) NOT null primary KEY,
      Name char(150),
      Age int);    then hit return
```

(i) Note varchar and char. The most important difference is that CHAR is padded with spaces and VARCHAR is not.

For example if code VARCHAR(2) and Name CHAR(2) and assign a single row the letter x, then when we retrieve that row then we get code = 'a ' and name = 'a' i.e. A space added to the right. This can be quite confusing for beginners when using such functions as LIKE.

Now when we type:
        SHOW TABLES;

we get a list of one table as shown below.

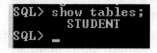

```
SQL> show tables;
          STUDENT
SQL> _
```

Creating tables will be dealt with in the next chapter.

# 4    Data Definition Language – DDL

*Creating and Manipulating Tables...*

The SQL Commands used for Creating and Manipulating Tables falls under the heading as a Data Defining Language (DDL).  In this chapter we will be looking at a few DDL commands for performing such tasks as creating, amending and deleting tables, etc.

## Creating Tables

We ended the previous chapter by creating a table to store information about students. In this chapter we will expand on the 'create table SQL' command along with other Table manipulation commands.

Let us re-examine the 'create table' command. *Recap:*

```
create table student (
   code varchar(20) NOT null primary KEY,
   Name char(150),
   Age int
);
```

The basic 'create table' syntax is as follows:

```
CREATE TABLE table_name (
      column1 datatype,
      column2 datatype,
      column3 datatype,
      ....
);
```

By issueing the 'create table' command as the name suggests to create a new table in our database and assign it the <u>unique</u> name student.

We then created a number of columns (each with <u>unique</u> names in the table) and specified the type of data that the column will hold.

Note that each column is separated by a comma except the last column, in our case the Age column. This signals the end of our column list, informing Firebird DBMS that this is the end of the column list and to expect the end closing bracket.

ⓘ In Firebird, to create a new table in your database, you must have the CREATE TABLE system privilege (user access rights, we will cover this at a later chapter of the book).

In our student table note the line:

```
code varchar(20) NOT null primary KEY,
```

First we create a column named *code* and allow it hold alphanumeric characters but we also restrict the number of characters it can hold to 20 with the use of *varchar(20),* the datatype constraint.
We further said that we want the column to be the primary key for the table and it cannot store null values.

ⓘ The **SQL NULL** is the term used to represent a missing value. A **NULL** value in a table is a value in a column that appears to be blank. A column with a **NULL** value is a column with no value. It is <u>very</u> <u>important</u> to understand that a **NULL** value is different to a zero value or a column that contains spaces.

Our second column we created is the 'Name' column: this column can also hold alphanumeric characters but this time we defined its datatype using the *char* operand, in this case 150 characters.
As mentioned previously there is a difference between varchar and char.

Our final column we created was the 'Age' with a datatype restriction of integer values only with the use of the *int* operand.

Now that we have created our Student Table, we can take a look at it by typing the following:

> show table student; *then hit return*

The following should result, listing the column names and datatype.

```
SQL> show table student;
CODE                              VARCHAR(20) Nullable
NAME                              CHAR(20) Nullable
AGE                               INTEGER Nullable
SQL>
```

*Use **select** to list data content of the table.*

We will be revisiting the SELECT command in depth in further chapters but for now let us have a brief introduction to the SQL SELECT command. The Select command is used to retrieve data from the database.

For now we will simply use it to list the content of our Student table.

Type the following:

```
SELECT * FROM student;  then hit return
```

**explaination...**
    We are using this statement to show *all records in all columns*. Note **\*** is known as a wildcard for all columns.

ⓘ A word of warning, when you are developing for production the wildcard should be used sparingly if at all. Only retrieve the necessary data you need, that is to say the columns you need and apply filters to your search. No point in retrieving 2GB of data if all you want was his/her mobile number.

Now back to our 'select' statement, you should get nothing in return. This is because we have not yet inserted any data into our Student table.

But before we do that there are still some amendments we should make to our student table. Code, Name and Age hardly tells us much at a glance. At the very least we should be able to contact the student. Let's amend the Student table to allow us to store ***Address, postcode/Zipcode, email, phoneNo.***

*Column/Field...*
In previous chapters and this chapter so far we have used the term column(s) however in some textbooks it is common to see columns referred to as fields. In this book we may sometime interchange the two. We will be doing this intentionally to let the beginner become familiar with the terms.

Now we will get back to the job at hand.

We will begin by adding an *Address* column to the student table. To do this type the following:

```
ALTER TABLE STUDENT ADD ADDRESS CHAR(250);
```
*then hit return*

The statement reads, *'Alter the **student** table by adding a column name **Address** of **Char** type to hold no more that **250** alphanumeric characters'*.

We should now add the post/zip code. Type the following:

```
ALTER TABLE STUDENT ADD POSTZIP CHAR(50)
DEFAULT '' NOT NULL;
```
*then hit return*

This statement is similar to our Address addition however in this case we are instructing Firebird to create a Postzip field and that this field can not contain a null value. It must contain something even if it is '' Therefore we enter a default value ''.

Now go ahead and add email and phoneno fields

```
ALTER TABLE STUDENT ADD EMAIL CHAR(150);
```
*then hit return*
```
ALTER TABLE STUDENT ADD PHONENO CHAR(150);
```
*then hit return*

Now let us take a look at what changes we have performed, Type the following:

```
show table student;
```
*then hit return*

You should have the following:

```
SQL> show table student;
CODE                              VARCHAR(20) Nullable
NAME                              CHAR(20) Nullable
AGE                               INTEGER Nullable
ADDRESS                           CHAR(250) Nullable
POSTZIP                           CHAR(50) Not Null default ''
EMAIL                             CHAR(150) Nullable
PHONENO                           CHAR(150) Nullable
SQL>
```

If we look at the Address column, having a character limit of 250 maybe too small therefore we may want to increase the size to 300. We can simply do this by typing the following:

```
ALTER TABLE STUDENT ALTER ADDRESS TYPE
CHAR(300);
```
*then hit return*

Note this time we replace *ADD* with *ALTER*

Now take a look, type:

```
show table student;
```
*then hit return*

You should have the following:

```
SQL> alter table student alter address type char(300);
SQL> show table student;
CODE                            VARCHAR(20) Nullable
NAME                            CHAR(20) Nullable
AGE                             INTEGER Nullable
ADDRESS                         CHAR(300) Nullable
POSTZIP                         CHAR(50) Not Null default ''
EMAIL                           CHAR(150) Nullable
PHONENO                         CHAR(150) Nullable
SQL> _
```

### create table using select...

If you are migrating from another RDBMS one obstacle that beginners constantly ask is:
*'Does Firebird support creating tables using the SELECT statement?'*

Unfortunately Firebird does not support this, at the time of writing this book.

ⓘ There are ways to achieve this in Firebird with a two stage approach: create table then use select query to populate. (With DBeaver you can click on the DDL tab to copy and rename the new table you wish to create from an existing table then simply INSERT INTO <table> SELECT * FROM,copied table>)

Another point that is worth mentioning also, is that most popular RDBMS support the following SQL:

```
CREATE TABLE IF NOT EXISTS testtable (
        `col` VARCHAR(16) NOT NULL
    );
```

```
Or

DROP TABLE IF EXISTS Product;
```

Firebird achieves this by using the PSQL feature EXECUTE Block statements. This is worth knowing but will not be used in this getting started book.

Despite these minor shortfalls, Firebird is still a great RDBMS system to use. Let us continue.

To delete a table from that database we simply issue the DROP command (assuming we know the table exists) we simply type *DROP TABLE tablename;*

We will end this chapter with a short list of things for you to try.

d i y *Things to try…*

1/ Create a table with the name substudent, with column id of integer type.
2/ Amend that substudent table by adding another field title of char type limit its dimension to 3 characters.
3/ Alter the substudent table field title column by increasing its field size to 6 characters.
4/ Delete the table from the database.

# 5 Firebird Data Manipulation Language (DML)

In the previous chapter we looked at a set of SQL commands that are considered as data definition language (DDL). In the next few chapters we will be looking a set of SQL commands that are considered to be data manipulation language (DML) commands.

We can best illustrate an overview of the SQL command categories as follows.

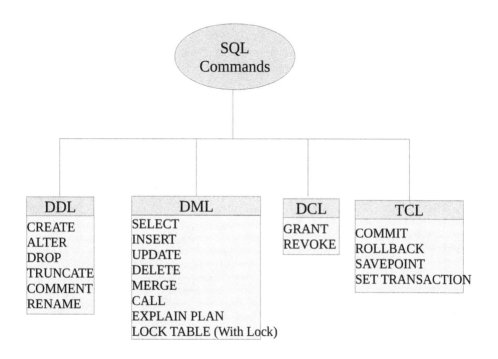

DCL: Date Control Language.

TCL: Transaction Control Language

## Quick DML overview...

**SELECT**

    FIRST, SKIP

    The SELECT Columns List

    The FROM clause

    Joins

    The WHERE clause

    The GROUP BY clause

    The PLAN clause

    UNION

    ORDER BY

    ROWS

    FOR UPDATE [OF]

    WITH LOCK

    INTO

    Common Table Expressions ("WITH ... AS ... SELECT")

**UPDATE**

    Using an alias

    The SET Clause

    The WHERE Clause

    The ORDER BY and ROWS Clauses

    The RETURNING Clause

    Updating BLOB columns

**UPDATE OR INSERT**

    The RETURNING clause

**INSERT**

    INSERT ... VALUES

    INSERT ... SELECT

    INSERT ... DEFAULT VALUES

    The RETURNING clause

    Inserting into BLOB columns

**DELETE**

    Aliases

    WHERE

    PLAN

    ORDER BY and ROWS

    RETURNING

**MERGE**
**EXECUTE PROCEDURE**

    "Executable" Stored Procedure

**EXECUTE BLOCK**

    Input and output parameters

    Statement Terminators

# 6   Inserting Data

In chapter three we created our Student table. Now we need to place information (insert data) into the table. In this chapter we will be looking at various ways of achieving that.

When we wish to add data to our table we use the INSERT command. Using the 'insert' command we can:
- Insert a whole row of data.
- Insert a few fields of data.
- Insert more than one row of data and
- Insert data from the results of a 'select' query.

### INSERT Syntax...

*INSERT INTO table_name (column1, column2, column3, ...)*
*VALUES (value1, value2, value3, ...);*

Let us now insert data into our Student table. Use the **'Show Table Student;'** command, to remind yourself of the fields held within our Student table.

```
SQL> alter table student alter address type char(300);
SQL> show table student;
CODE                      VARCHAR(20) Nullable
NAME                      CHAR(20) Nullable
AGE                       INTEGER Nullable
ADDRESS                   CHAR(300) Nullable
POSTZIP                   CHAR(50) Not Null default ''
EMAIL                     CHAR(150) Nullable
PHONENO                   CHAR(150) Nullable
SQL> _
```

### Inserting a whole row...

Type the following:

```
INSERT INTO STUDENT
(CODE,NAME,AGE,ADDRESS,POSTZIP,EMAIL,PHONENO)
        VALUES ('SK765','John Smith',19,'123456 Pitts
Avenue','IO98        76X','j.smith@xyz.com','071234566');
```

There are a few points worth noting here. First to enter data of datatype char or varchar you must place the data in between quotes. Most RDBMS accept single quotes (') some double (") Throughout this book we will be using single quotes.

Another point to mention is that datatypes like integer, float etc, i.e. numbers you insert without the need for quotes.

Now that we have inserted our first row of data, we can now take a look at it by using our select query statement as mentioned previously.

Type the following;

SELECT * FROM STUDENT; *then hit return*

You should get the following;

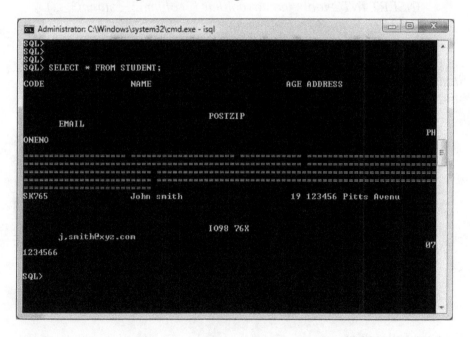

The way the screen looks is not very attractive, but we can identify the data we inserted into our student table.

Now, if we were to continue inserting more data, the listing would become fairly difficult to read for experienced programmers, let alone the beginner. It is at this point we will switch to a graphical user interface (GUI) tool to aid in our learning and understanding.

*Using a GUI Tool...*

The command prompt utility can perform all the necessary tasks needed for setting up, configuring and maintaining Firebird. This is the preferred tool used by professional database administrators. However, when learning about databases, it is sometimes easier to use a graphical user interface tool. As mentioned earlier there is a wealth of GUI tools for managing Firebird.

This chapter we recommend that you install DBeaver.

We will be connecting DBeaver to our database via Open Database Connectivity (ODBC).

### *Setting ODBC...*

Download and install Firebird ODBC Driver. You can obtain it from the following website:

https://www.firebirdsql.org/en/odbc-driver/

In our example we will install the windows 64bit version.

Once installed we will need to setup a connection.

In the windows search bar type ODBC and select Data Source (ODBC) as shown below.

You should be presented with the following screen:

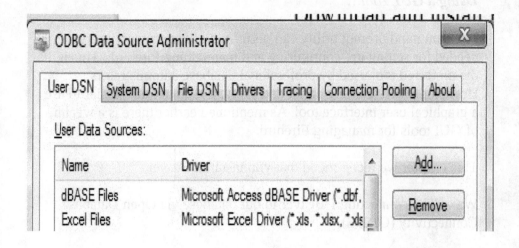

Click on the Add button and select Firebird/InterBase(r) driver, as shown below:

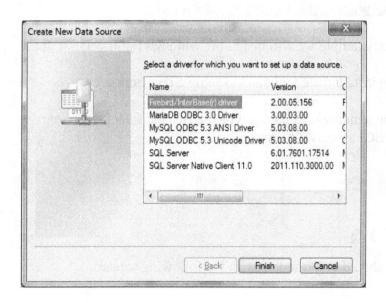

then Click Finish.

Populate the screen as shown below:

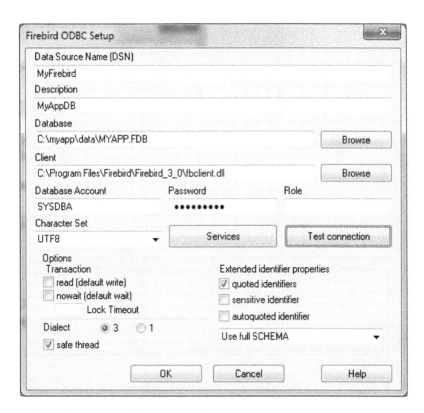

remember the password is *masterkey*

Test the connection by clicking the Test connection button. If successful you should get the following screen.

If it fails then it maybe that you still have isql.exe still running. Close isql.exe and try again.

Now we have an ODBC connection setup we can use it with any program. In this case DBbeaver.

So let's now install and setup Dbeaver.

*Installing DBeaver...*

Download DBeaver from http://dbeaver.jkiss.org/download/

Note that DBeaver requires java version 1.6 or higher. For Windows users this is included in the installation but for other users you may need to install java first.

For Windows users simply choose the installation that matches your system and install.

For Linux and Mac users (assuming that you have java 1.6 or higher installed), download the relevant DBbeaver zip file and extract it into a folder.

Next click on the DBeaver icon. That's it!

When running DBeaver for the first time you will be presented with a dialog window requesting which database DBMS type you wish to connect to. Select your database ODBC as shown below:

Click the 'Next' button and enter the following parameters:

Click the Test Connection button. If ok then click the next button.

Then 'next' then finally click the finish button.

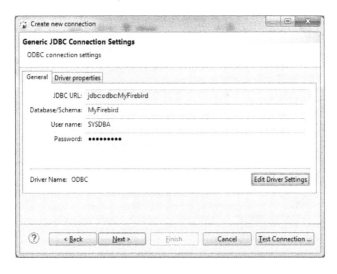

Right mouse-click on ODBC - MyFirebird and select refresh as shown below

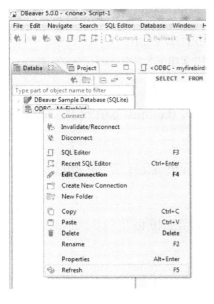

You should now have connection to our database. As shown below.

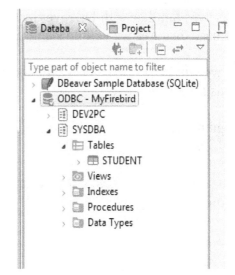

We can now test our connection.

Double click on the *STUDENT* table and you should have a screen similar to the one shown below.

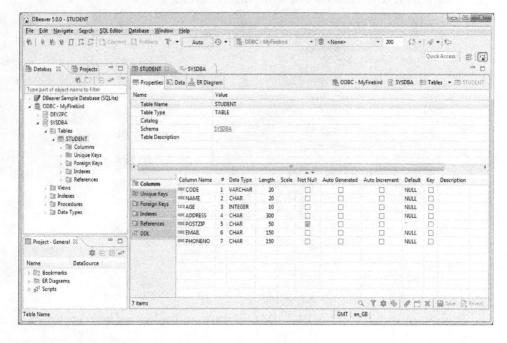

***Quick Tour of DBeaver…***

Before we delve back into exploring Firebird it would pay to get ourselves familiar with DBeaver by taking a quick tour just to cover the basic features we will be using.

As we will be using the DBeaver console for the most part of the book let us set this up next.

Right mouse-click on the STUDENT table and select *'Read data in SQL console'*

You should be presented with the screen similarly to the one shown below:

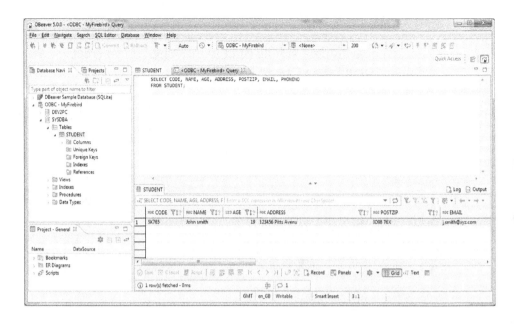

This has created a select query and executed it for us showing the
result below. We will be re-using this console to execute all our
queries. Note how the result is presented in a more readable style than
our *isql* console.

We will be coming back to this console shortly, but for now switch
back to the STUDENT screenshot presented previously.

We begin our tour by taking a look at the section below

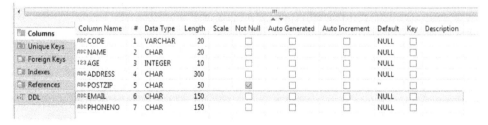

The various tabs allow you to carry out Table manipulation
graphically:
table Columns allow you to Add, Setup, Delete or Amend Columns in
a table.

## *Adding and Removing a Column...*

To add a new column simple right mouse click on an empty
cell below and select **Create New Column**

Make your entries and click the save icon
(button right)

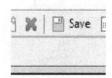

Once you have clicked the Save icon you will be presented
with the screenshot shown below:

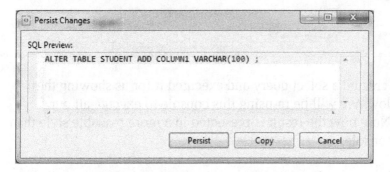

Notice that the SQL statement is written for you. This is a great way to learn
SQL syntax, as you continue to create more complex queries in the future.

Click the Persist button to commit changes.

To delete the column, simply right mouse click on the column name
you wish to remove and select delete, again click save to commit.

## *Adding a Unique Key...*

Select the Unique Key tab. Now right mouse-click anywhere
on a blank section of the grid and select Create New Unique
Key. As shown below.

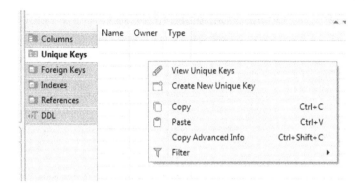

The following screen should be presented as shown below:

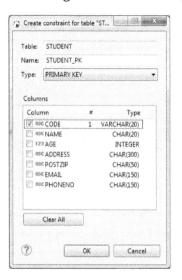

If the CODE field is not checked then check it and click OK

The other tabs we will leave for now except DDL (Table Data Definition Language) Select the DDL tab.

This will reveal the SQL Editor (F3 key) that would have created the table if we did it manually as shown below:

```
CREATE TABLE STUDENT (
    CODE VARCHAR(20) DEFAULT NULL,
    NAME CHAR(20) DEFAULT NULL,
    AGE INTEGER DEFAULT NULL,
    ADDRESS CHAR(300) DEFAULT NULL,
    POSTZIP CHAR(50) DEFAULT ' ' NOT NULL,
    EMAIL CHAR(150) DEFAULT NULL,
    PHONENO CHAR(150) DEFAULT NULL,
    CONSTRAINT PRIMARY KEY (CODE) CONSTRAINT STUDENT_PK
) ;
```

We now turn our attention to the upper section, see below:

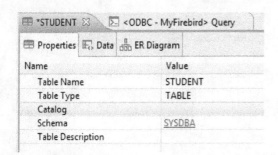

The Student properties tab gives us information about the table such as Name Type and Schema.

Now click the Student Data tab. You should have a screen similar to the one shown below:

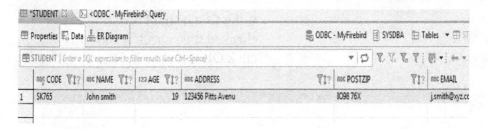

This shows you the data held in the table.

Now click the ER – Diagram tab. You should have a screen similar to the one shown below:

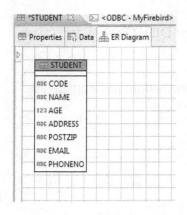

This will show you a graphical representation of the relationship between the tables in our database.

ER = Entity - Relationship

That concludes our very brief tour of our DBbeaver GUI tool. However as you progress through the book you will be introduced to more key features of DBeaver.

So now click back to our ODBC MyFirebird <query> console tab and we will continue where we left off inserting data into our Student table.

Note to execute your SQL command you need to click the ***Execute SQL statement*** button see below

## Inserting Data (Records) over multiple lines...

It is common practice to refer to a row of data in a table as a record. Therefore we will adopt this convention.

The DBeaver console allows us to place multiple statements in one batch before executing the query. Enter the following in the console:

Then click the ***execute script*** button

If you have entered the insert statement correctly you should have a screen similar to the one presented below:

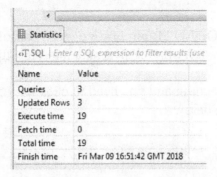

You can now view the records entered by simply clicking the STUDENT Data tab

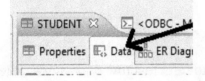

Then right-mouse click the grid below the first record and select refresh or simply press the F5 function key on your keyboard.

This will refresh the page. You should see a similar screen as shown below:

ⓘ Note that when using **INSERT** the column names/data-type as well as the number of columns listed must match, for example let's say col1 is a number only column and col2 = text value then:

INSERT (col1, col2) VALUES ("John", 23); would *fail* because col1 was expecting a number value

INSERT (col1, col2) VALUES (23, "John", "123"); this would also *fail* as the insert was expecting only two columns of information;

INSERT (col1, col2) VALUES (23, John); This would also *fail* as col2 expects a text value in quotes.

INSERT (col1,col2) VALUES (23, "John"); This statement is correct.

*Inserting records from a SELECT query...*

In the previous section we looked at recording information into our Student table using **INSERT** and **VALUES** statement. We also showed how multiple lines can be contained within a single script.

However there are times when you need to insert data from the result of a query. Firebird supports this.

To demonstrate this we need to a create a table with a few columns.

Type the following and execute the script:

```
create table substudent (
  code varchar(20) NOT null primary KEY,
  Name char(150),
  Age int
);
```

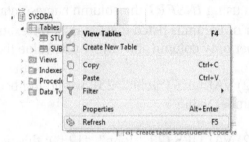

Now right-mouse click the Tables and select refresh.

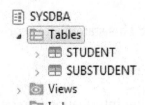

We have now created another table in our database called substudent.

Now delete the 'create table' script, type and execute the following SQL statement:

```
INSERT INTO substudent (CODE, NAME,AGE) SELECT CODE,NAME,Age
FROM Student;
```

Now view the substudent table you will see a similar screen as presented below.

| ABC CODE | ABC NAME | 123 AGE |
|---|---|---|
| SK765 | John smith | 19 |
| PH856 | Peter Hollis | 19 |
| FL065 | Fiona Jones | 20 |
| JH321 | Jane Headly | 21 |

It is rare that you would want to copy an entire list from one table into another, it is usually the case that you would only wish to copy a subset of data from one table to the other. In other words, we need to set some form of criteria that will allow us to select the records we wish to copy. We achieve this by using the 'where' clause.

### Using the 'where clause...

In order for us to select the required records we need, SQL has a *where* mechanism that allows you to filter the data you want to include or ignore from your result.

This time we will create another table and only insert records based on some sort of criteria.

Do the following: create a table called myStudent with two columns, '*code*' and '*Name*' both data-type.

```
create table myStudent (
    code varchar(20) NOT null primary KEY,
    Name char(150)
);
```

Refresh the Tables list and now see the myStudent table listed. By double-clicking on myStudent you will see the table data view with no records entered yet.

To demonstrate how we use the '**where**' clause, we can do so under various criteria. We will be looking in depth at the 'select' query in later chapters. But for now we will look at two examples..

### Inserting a single record based on identifying the required record...

We can simply use the primary key to identify the actual record we wish to insert into our table.

Type the following and execute the SQL query;

```
INSERT INTO myStudent (CODE, NAME) SELECT CODE,NAME
FROM Student WHERE CODE='PH856';
```

Now go and inspect the myStudent table, you should have a display similarly to the one shown below.

You should find that the myStudent table contains a single student entry.

59

*Inserting multiple records based on exclusion...*

Type the following and execute the SQL query;

```
INSERT INTO myStudent (CODE, NAME) SELECT CODE,NAME
FROM Student WHERE age > 19;
```

Now re-inspect the myStudent table (remember to refresh the table to see changes each time).

This criteria excludes any student aged 19yrs and below.

Note that the table added two more entries to the table, making three entries, one from the previous single entry query and two from our previous query.

There are numerous combinations we could have applied to the filtering to achieve our goal. These combinations will be discussed in later chapters in the book.

[d][i][y]*Things to try...*

1/ Insert two student records into the student table.
2/ create a table based on the substudent table and insert data derived from resultant querying the substudent table.

# 7   Updating and Deleting Data

In chapter 6 we looked at various ways we can insert data into tables. In this chapter we will look at how data that already exist, can be changed or removed from the table.

To change values in our table **SQL** provides the **UPDATE** statement and the **SET** clause.

The basic syntax example is as follows:

```
UPDATE <TableName>
SET <Column2> = 'SK098', <Column3>='Alfred Holmes'
WHERE <Column1> = 1;
```

(i) Word of WARNING

When performing an Update operation it is good practice to first construct a 'select' query with the filters you require, check the result of your select is the list you require, then use that filter as part of your update query operation.

Another good practice is to backup before update. This is usually if you are about to change tens of thousands (or even millions) of records.

In the above example, if you forget to include the '**where**' filter, then ALL the records in the table will have column2 and column3 set to the values above.

There are times when you will want to do a blanket update which then would be okay to omit the **WHERE** filter.

To demonstrate using the Update statement type the following and execute the query:

```
UPDATE substudent
SET AGE = 22
WHERE CODE = 'PH856';
```

Now if you re-inspect the **substudent** table you will notice that student *Peter Hollis* is now aged 22 in the **substudent** table but is still age 19 **Student** table.
Updating multiple columns in one operation…

We can change more than one column in one statement for eaxmple:

```
UPDATE substudent
SET AGE = 23, NAME='Peter Hollis Davison'
WHERE CODE = 'PH856';
```

Type the above and re-inspect the **substudent** table. You should have a similar screen as shown below.

*Deleting records from a table...*

There are times when you no longer need to keep records in a table and for this, SQL provides the Delete command.

ⓘ The same word of WARNING applies to the **DELETE** operation as it does to the **UPDATE** *(test before delete, backup and apply filter).*

Syntax for Delete

DELETE FROM <table> WHERE <filter>;

for example, let's say that we wish to remove 'Jane Headly' from our **substudent** table.

We simply type and execute the following statement:

```
DELETE FROM substudent WHERE CODE='JH321';
```

Now if you refresh the substudent table you should notice that 'Jane Headly' is no longer listed in the **substudent** table.

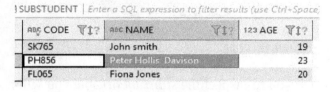

ⓘ Note that without the '**WHERE**' clause the entire table would be wiped clean of all its records. There are times when this is necessary, but do so cautiously.

# Summing up chapters 3 to 6

### Getting Started with Firebird...

In chapter 3 we start now to get more involved with Firebird. We connected to the myapp.fdb database that we created in the previous chapter. We delved further into Firebird's isql command-line tool, which we used to create our student table.

### Creating and Manipulating data...

In this chapter we showed how to Alter existing tables. We looked more closely at the **ALTER** command, along with Columns and there Data-type. We ended this chapter by looking at how to remove a table from the database using the **DROP** command.

### Inserting Data...

This chapter focused on getting data into the table. This chapter showed how by using the **INSERT INTO** command we can push data into our tables.

As this book is aimed at beginners and intermediate users the isql command-line tool can be a little overwhelming. For this we recommended the reader to download and install the free open source DBeaver database graphical user interface (GUI) tool. This allows a more intuitive approach to the reader's learning. Once DBeaver was installed we took a very brief tour of the tool, familiarizing ourselves with some of the basics. Once we were fairly familiar with DBeaver we continued our investigation on the INSERT command using the DBeaver console feature and checking the results,

### Updating and Deleting Data...

Once we have inserted your data into our tables, over time that data held within the table needs to be updated or removed. This chapter introduced the **UPDATE..SET** command along with the **WHERE** clause for identifying the required record we wished to make changes to.

We also took a look in this chapter at how to remove data from a table with the use of the **DELETE** command.

# 8  Retrieving Data

In earlier chapters we casually used the *select* command as a means to support the previous commands.

However by far the most used SQL command is the **SELECT** command. A large portion of the rest of the book will be devoted to looking and understanding how we use the *select* command to retrieve data from one or more tables. Consider the following:

Retrieving All Columns and All Data from a table...
To retrieve everything from a table we simply type and execute the SQL statement below:

```
SELECT * FROM student;
```

This will retrieve the entire content of the *student* table. Notice the wild card (*) which means include all the columns for the table. As mentioned earlier and to re-iterate here again, Such a Query comes at a cost, in performance and user experience if the table holds millions of records. Therefore also aim to construct your retrieve queries to only retrieve the data you require, use filters and only include the columns you require.

### Sorting the data...
The above query will return the data in any order, usually in the order that it was recorded, in the table.
We can amend our simple query to sort our result by a particular column and whether we want the list to be in ascending or descending order.

Consider the following:

```
SELECT * FROM student ORDER BY CODE;
```

Result:

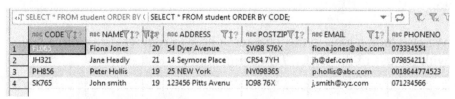

| | CODE | NAME | | ADDRESS | POSTZIP | EMAIL | PHONENO |
|---|---|---|---|---|---|---|---|
| 1 | FLO65 | Fiona Jones | 20 | 54 Dyer Avenue | SW98 S76X | fiona.jones@abc.com | 073334554 |
| 2 | JH321 | Jane Headly | 21 | 14 Seymore Place | CR54 7YH | jh@def.com | 079854211 |
| 3 | PH856 | Peter Hollis | 19 | 25 NEW York | NY098365 | p.hollis@abc.com | 0018644774523 |
| 4 | SK765 | John smith | 19 | 123456 Pitts Avenu | IO98 76X | j.smith@xyz.com | 071234566 |

The resultant query now lists the record, sorted by the CODE column. Note that this sort is in ascending order. Most RDBMS default ordering to ASCENDING however the following is just as valid in Firebird,

```
SELECT * FROM student ORDER BY CODE ASCENDING;

SELECT * FROM student ORDER BY CODE ASC;
```

The above two are valid in Firebird, however most RDBMS uses *ASC* for ascending.

For descending we simply write the following:

```
SELECT * FROM student ORDER BY CODE DESC;    OR

SELECT * FROM student ORDER BY CODE DESCENDING;
```

You can also sort by multiple columns but the ordering is important: that is first come first serve, so to speak, i.e. sort by col1 then col2 the col3, etc.

So we could write the following:

```
SELECT * FROM student ORDER BY Age, CODE ASC;
```

Result:

| CODE | NAME | AGE | ADDRESS | POSTZIP | EMAIL | PHONENO |
|------|------|-----|---------|---------|-------|---------|
| JH656 | Peter Hollis | 19 | 25 NEW York | NY098365 | p.hollis@abc.com | 0018644774523 |
| SK765 | John smith | 19 | 123456 Pitts Avenu | IO98 76X | j.smith@xyz.com | 071234566 |
| FL065 | Fiona Jones | 20 | 54 Dyer Avenue | SW98 S76X | fiona.jones@abc.com | 073334554 |
| JH321 | Jane Headly | 21 | 14 Seymore Place | CR54 7YH | jh@def.com | 079854211 |

Note that The AGE column takes precedence followed by the code sort. Now consider the following:

```
SELECT * FROM student ORDER BY AGE, NAME ASC;
```

Result:

| ᴀʙᴄ CODE ↑? | ᴀʙᴄ NAME ↑? | ↑? | ᴀʙᴄ ADDRESS ↑? | ᴀʙᴄ POSTZ↑? | ᴀʙᴄ EMAIL ↑? | ᴀʙᴄ PHONENO |
|---|---|---|---|---|---|---|
| SK765 | John smith | 19 | 123456 Pitts Avenu | IO98 76X | j.smith@xyz.com | 071234566 |
| PH856 | Peter Hollis | 19 | 25 NEW York | NY098365 | p.hollis@abc.com | 0018644774523 |
| FL065 | Fiona Jones | 20 | 54 Dyer Avenue | SW98 S76X | fiona.jones@abc.com | 073334554 |
| JH321 | Jane Headly | 21 | 14 Seymore Place | CR54 7YH | jh@def.com | 079854211 |

Note this time AGE still take precedence but now followed by NAME.

### *Retrieve data with selected columns...*

We can have our *select* query return the result in any column order we wish. Type the following:

```
SELECT NAME, POSTZIP, CODE FROM student ORDER BY AGE,
NAME ASC;
```

Result:

SELECT NAME, POSTZIP, CODE FRO | *Enter a SQL e*

| ᴀʙᴄ NAME ↑? | ᴀʙᴄ POSTZIP ↑? | ᴀʙᴄ CODE |
|---|---|---|
| John smith | IO98 76X | SK765 |
| Peter Hollis | NY098365 | PH856 |
| Fiona Jones | SW98 S76X | FL065 |
| Jane Headly | CR54 7YH | JH321 |

Notice we do not need to list the columns to sort with them. In this query we only wanted to list three columns in a particular order.

In terms of hardware overheads we only retrieve the columns we are interested in therefore reducing the performance overheads. However we can improve on this by further applying some sort of filter, i.e. retrieving the data based on some sort of criteria, with the use of the **WHERE** clause we introduced in previous chapters.

### *Filtering our search...*

By using the **where** clause we can reduce our list from al records to a subset of records.

Type the following and execute the query:

```
SELECT NAME, POSTZIP, CODE FROM student WHERE AGE=19
ORDER BY AGE, NAME ASC;
```

you should get the following:

SELECT NAME, POSTZIP, CODE FRO | *Enter a SQL ex*

| ABC NAME ▼‡? | ABC POSTZIP ▼‡? | ABC CODE |
|---|---|---|
| John smith | IO98 76X | SK765 |
| Peter Hollis | NY098365 | PH856 |

The results show that we have only two students aged 19 in our *student* table.

Consider the following, before typing in the following, what do you think the result will be?

```
SELECT NAME, POSTZIP, CODE FROM student WHERE AGE BETWEEN 19
AND 20 ORDER BY AGE, NAME ASC;
```

I won't list that answer, you can see for yourself.

### Filtering using LIKE and it's "%" wildcard...

Firebird has a very useful Filter operand feature that allows you to perform pattern matching on the text data-type. We will take a closer look at how we can use the LIKE condition search and how to avoid common problems.

Type the following and execute the statement:

```
SELECT NAME,POSTZIP,CODE, AGE FROM student WHERE NAME
LIKE('%n%');
```

Result: The query retrieves students who have the letter 'n' anywhere in their name.

SELECT NAME,POSTZIP,CODE, AGE | *Enter a SQL expression to filter result*

| ABC NAME ▼‡? | ABC POSTZIP ▼‡? | ABC COD▼‡? | 123 AGE▼‡? |
|---|---|---|---|
| John smith | IO98 76X | SK765 | 19 |
| Fiona Jones | SW98 S76X | FL065 | 20 |
| Jane Headly | CR54 7YH | JH321 | 21 |

Consider the following:

```
SELECT NAME,POSTZIP,CODE, AGE FROM student WHERE NAME
LIKE('J%');
```

Result:

This query retrieves students who's names begin with the letter 'J'

| ABC NAME ⍦↕? | ABC POSTZIP ⍦↕? | ABC CODE ⍦↕? | 123 AGE ⍦↕? |
|---|---|---|---|
| John smith | IO98 76X | SK765 | 19 |
| Jane Headly | CR54 7YH | JH321 | 21 |

### Common problem areas for beginners

Consider the following:

```
SELECT NAME,POSTZIP,CODE, AGE FROM student WHERE NAME
LIKE('j%');
```

Result:

> The result here is nothing, because the **LIKE**
> condition is case-sensitive 'j' is not the same
> as 'J'. Default Firebird is case-sensitive.

| ABC NAME ⍦↕? | ABC POSTZIP ⍦↕? | ABC CODE ⍦↕? | 123 AGE ⍦↕? |
|---|---|---|---|
| | | | |

to include both uppercase and lowercase letters we simply write the following:

```
SELECT NAME,POSTZIP,CODE, AGE FROM student WHERE NAME
LIKE('j%') OR NAME LIKE('J%');
```

With the use of the **OR** operator.

ⓘ We could use the **CONTAINING** keyword, but more on that in chapter 9.

Another common problem that beginners come across, can best be demonstrated as follows:

first let's look at our full list of students again.

| ABC NAME | ABC POSTZIP | ABC CODE | 123 AGE |
|---|---|---|---|
| John smith | IO98 76X | SK765 | 19 |
| Peter Hollis | NY098365 | PH856 | 19 |
| Fiona Jones | SW98 S76X | FL065 | 20 |
| Jane Headly | CR54 7YH | JH321 | 21 |

Now we want to list any student who's name ends with '**th**', in our example that would be '***John Smith***'

So it would be reasonable to write the following:

```
SELECT NAME,POSTZIP,CODE, AGE FROM student WHERE NAME
LIKE('%th'); and expect John Smith to be listed.
```

What you get in return instead is nothing:

This is because the NAME column is a data-type CHAR.(20)

Because the NAME column is a data-type of CHAR this means that the column has spaces trailing to make up the character length of the field. Therefore now type that following:

```
SELECT NAME,POSTZIP,CODE, AGE FROM student WHERE NAME
LIKE('%th          ');
```

The result will be as we expect:

| ABC NAME | ABC POSTZIP | ABC | 123 AGE |
|---|---|---|---|
| John smith | IO98 76X | SK765 | 19 |

'John Smith' is 10 characters, when we pad out the rest of the column with 10 spaces we get our result.

Clearly this is undesirable, however we can resolve this problem by using the TRIM command to remove leading or trailing spaces from a text field.

Type the following and execute the statement:

```
SELECT NAME,POSTZIP,CODE, AGE FROM student WHERE
TRIM(NAME) LIKE('%th');
```

The TRIM function removes leading and/or trailing spaces.

Result:

SELECT NAME,POSTZIP,CODE, AGE | Enter a SQL expression to filter

| ABC NAME | ABC POSTZIP | ABC | 123 AGE |
|----------|-------------|-----|---------|
| John smith | IO98 76X | SK765 | 19 |

Retrieving Distinct Rows...
Consider the following

```
SELECT AGE FROM student;
```

This will list all Ages in the Student table as follows:

SELECT AGE FROM s

| 123 AGE |
|---------|
| 19 |
| 19 |
| 20 |
| 21 |

All ages are listed

Now what if you only want a list of distinct values. Well we can use the DISTINCT keyword to instruct Firebird to return only distinct records.

Type the following:

```
SELECT DISTINCT AGE FROM student;
```

| 123 AGE |
|---------|
| 19 |
| 20 |
| 21 |

Result: Only distinct values are returned.
Note The Distinct keyword must be placed directly in front of the column name.

## *Limiting your Results...*

There are times when you are only interest in the first few records, for example the top two oldest students in the student table.

First let's produce our full ordered list.

```
SELECT  * FROM student ORDER BY AGE DESC;
```

| | ABC CODE | ABC NAME | 123 AGE | ABC ADDRESS | ABC POSTZIP | ABC EMAIL | ABC PHONENO |
|---|---|---|---|---|---|---|---|
| 1 | JH321 | Jane Headly | 21 | 14 Seymore Place | CR54 7YH | jh@def.com | 079854211 |
| 2 | FL065 | Fiona Jones | 20 | 54 Dyer Avenue | SW98 S76X | fiona.jones@abc.com | 073334554 |
| 3 | PH856 | Peter Hollis | 19 | 25 NEW York | NY098365 | p.hollis@abc.com | 0018644774523 |
| 4 | SK765 | John smith | 19 | 123456 Pitts Avenu | IO98 76X | j.smith@xyz.com | 071234566 |

In firebird we can limit our result as follows:

```
SELECT FIRST 2 * FROM student ORDER BY AGE DESC;
```

Result:

Consider the following:

```
SELECT FIRST 2 Skip 1 * FROM student ORDER BY AGE DESC;
```

Result:

| ABC COD | ABC NAME | 123 AGE | ABC ADDRESS | ABC POSTZIP | ABC EMAIL | ABC PHONENO |
|---|---|---|---|---|---|---|
| FL065 | Fiona Jones | 20 | 54 Dyer Avenue | SW98 S76X | fiona.jones@abc.com | 073334554 |
| PH856 | Peter Hollis | 19 | 25 NEW York | NY098365 | p.hollis@abc.com | 0018644774523 |

In this example we still limit our list to two records but this time we skipped the first record.

The syntax is basically:

... FIRST x SKIP n ,<col,c..,> ...

SKIP n  Instructs Firebird to skip n number of records before starting its query returns.

### *Using Fully Qualified Table Names...*

Up until now we have been working with a single table therefore we have been using shortcuts when constructing our SQL statements.

Now SQL allows you to construct a single statement using multiple tables, and some tables may have the same column names. Therefore we need to instruct Firebird which table we are referring to, to retrieve required column data.

We do this by using Fully Qualified table names, for example the dot operator is used.

```
SELECT Student.CODE, Student.Name FROM student ORDER BY
AGE DESC;
```

Result:

| ABC CODE ▼↕? | ABC NAME ▼ |
|--------------|------------|
| JH321 | Jane Headly |
| FL065 | Fiona Jones |
| PH856 | Peter Hollis |
| SK765 | John smith |

Using fully qualified table names adds clarity to the SQL statement.

### *Using Comments...*

Although SQL was designed to be fairly clean and descriptive in its construction there are times you wish to add comments to your script to help other members of staff to understand the script but at the same time instruct Firebird to ignore your comments.

Firebird allows you the ability to add human readable text to your SQL statement. Consider the following:

```
SELECT  Student.CODE, Student.Name
FROM student    -- This is an in-line comment
ORDER BY AGE DESC;
```

Also consider the following:

```
/*
 This
 is a
 Multiple
 Line
 Comment
 */
SELECT Student.CODE, Student.Name
FROM student   -- This is an in-line comment
ORDER BY AGE DESC;
```

# 9    Filtering the Data

In the previous chapter we briefly touched on the WHERE clause and a few operators to filter our data. In this chapter we will take a closer look into the various ways we can filter our data.

As was mentioned previously, you seldom need to retrieve all the data in a table. More often you only want a subset. Retrieving just the data you want requires you to specify some sort of search criteria, in other words, you need to apply a filter condition to your search. This is where the **WHERE** ('no pun intended') comes into play.

*Using the* WHERE *clause...*

Using a few examples should make it clear to the reader how the **WHERE** clause is used.

Type the following SQL statements. Use a single line comment to comment out all except the one you are working on. Execute each one separately by removing the '--' single line comment and note your results. *Example.*

```
--SELECT CODE, NAME FROM STUDENT WHERE CODE = 'SK765';
--SELECT CODE, NAME FROM STUDENT WHERE CODE = 'SK765' OR CODE = 'FL065';
--SELECT CODE, NAME, AGE FROM STUDENT WHERE AGE = 19;
--SELECT CODE, NAME, AGE FROM STUDENT WHERE AGE = 19 AND CODE <> 'PH856';
SELECT CODE, NAME, AGE FROM STUDENT WHERE AGE >= 19 AND CODE <> 'PH856';
--SELECT CODE, NAME, AGE FROM STUDENT WHERE AGE > 19 AND CODE <> 'PH856';
--SELECT CODE, NAME, AGE FROM STUDENT WHERE AGE BETWEEN 20 AND 21;
--SELECT CODE, NAME, AGE FROM STUDENT WHERE AGE > 19 AND AGE < 22;
--SELECT CODE, NAME, AGE FROM STUDENT WHERE CODE LIKE('%65');
--SELECT CODE, NAME, AGE FROM STUDENT WHERE CODE IS NOT NULL;
--SELECT CODE, NAME, AGE FROM STUDENT WHERE CODE IS NULL;
--SELECT CODE, NAME, AGE FROM STUDENT WHERE AGE IN (19, 21);
```

1. `SELECT CODE, NAME FROM STUDENT WHERE CODE = 'SK765';`

2. `SELECT CODE, NAME FROM STUDENT WHERE CODE = 'SK765' OR CODE = 'FL065';`

3. `SELECT CODE, NAME, AGE FROM STUDENT WHERE AGE = 19;`

4. `SELECT CODE, NAME, AGE FROM STUDENT WHERE AGE = 19 AND CODE <> 'PH856';`

5. `SELECT CODE, NAME, AGE FROM STUDENT WHERE AGE >= 19 AND CODE <> 'PH856';`

6. ```
SELECT CODE, NAME, AGE FROM STUDENT WHERE AGE > 19 AND
CODE <> 'PH856';
```

7. ```
SELECT CODE, NAME, AGE FROM STUDENT WHERE AGE BETWEEN
20 AND 21;
```

8. ```
SELECT CODE, NAME, AGE FROM STUDENT WHERE AGE > 19 AND
AGE < 22;
```

9. ```
SELECT CODE, NAME, AGE FROM STUDENT WHERE CODE
LIKE('%65');
```

10. ```
SELECT CODE, NAME, AGE FROM STUDENT WHERE CODE IS NOT
NULL;
```

11. ```
SELECT CODE, NAME, AGE FROM STUDENT WHERE CODE IS NULL;
```

12. ```
SELECT CODE, NAME, AGE FROM STUDENT WHERE AGE IN (19,
21);
```

13. ```
SELECT CODE, NAME, AGE FROM STUDENT WHERE CODE
LIKE('_K765');
```

In statements 1, 3 and 9 we are checking against a single value. One important point to note here is that in statement 9 we use the **LIKE** keyword, on the 'code' column, without the need for trimming any spaces or performing any space padding. The reason for this is that **CODE** is defined as a **VARCHAR** data-type, that is VARCHAR does not insert any space padding.

Statement 2, we are checking to see if there is a student whose code is **SK765 OR FL065.**
This statement uses the **OR** operator.
Note, in statements 4, 5, 6 that the second term uses the symbol <> to mean **Not Equal to.** In other words checking for no match. Whereas the symbol = means Equal to, i.e. checking for an exact match.

Statements 4, 5, 6, 7, 8 all use the **AND** operator to check against more than one column and if each term is 'true' then the operation will return a result. Note if any term fails (i.e. returns as 'false' ) then the whole statement fails.

Statement 6 also uses the symbol > i.e. the '*Greater than*' sign. Here we are checking for values greater than a given number value. Note using either > or < is usually used to check against number value datatype fields.

Statement 5 uses the symbol >= which reads Greater than <u>*or*</u> Equal to. Statements 7 and 8 are checking for a *Range of values*

You may have noticed that statements 7 and 8 say basically the same thing, but statement 7 looks a little neater.

Statements 10 and 11 are checking for 'no values'. Let's elaborate. When a table is created, the table designer can specify whether individual columns can contain 'no values' on creation of a record. When a column contains 'no values', we say that it contains a NULL value. This means we can check against a NULL value. So the idea of what looks like an empty field with nothing in it, is recognised in computing terms, as a field with a NULL value.
Therefore statement 10 checks to see for the code column that it does not contain a NULL value and statement 11 checks to see if the code column contains a NULL value.

Statement 12 uses the **IN** operator which checks a range of conditions as specified in the brackets.

Statement 13 uses the '_' (i.e. low dash), as a wildcard to match to a single character whereas '%' (i.e. percentage) wildcard is used to match any number of character patterns.

List of **WHERE** clause *operators*...

| Operator | Description |
|---|---|
| = | Equal to |
| <> | Not equal to |
| != | Not equal to – less commonly used in SQL statements |
| < | Less than |
| <= | Less than or equal to |
| > | Greater than |
| >= | Greater than or equal to |
| Between | Between two specified values |

| | |
|---|---|
| AND | More than one column is used is get a match |
| OR | Any column specified is used to get a match |
| IN | Checked a range of conditions specified IN the |
| brackets | |
| NOT | Negates whatever condition comes next. |

### Things to try...

1. Slightly modify statement 8 to also give the same results. Hint : look at the statement 5 first and the clause term.

2. Rewrite statement 2 using the IN operator.

3. Experiment with the '%' wildcard, for example see what the following resultant will be.

   ```
   SELECT CODE, NAME, AGE FROM STUDENT WHERE CODE
   LIKE('%6%');
   ```

4. Experiment with the '_' wildcard, for example see what the following resultant will be.

   ```
   SELECT CODE, NAME, AGE FROM STUDENT WHERE CODE
   LIKE('S_765');
   ```

# 10 Using Regular Expressions

As our filtering requirements become more complex, so does our **WHERE** clause increase in complexity.

This is where regular expressions come in to play. Regular expressions are used to perform text pattern matching. If you wanted to match part of a text we would use a regular expression. Remember, we first came across this when we used the LIKE operator (see filtering), but this had a number of drawbacks. Firstly it is case sensitive, secondly unless you use the wildcard then the whole text must be matched.

Consider if you wanted to to find a student whose name contains 'eter' But we are not sure how it is stored in the database: it could be typed in a variety of ways, such as eTeR, ETer, etER, etc.

Now if we were to use the LIKE operator then we could test a number of solutions:

1. We could perform a match on all possible combination and hoped we don't miss one.
2. We could convert to uppercase or lowercase and check accordingly for example:
   ```
   SELECT * FROM student WHERE UPPER(NAME) LIKE
   UPPER('%eTeR%');
   ```

This technique also has its limitations, one being not formatted correctly double spaced for two part name.

Or

We could use the special keyword *CONTAINING* for example:

```
SELECT * FROM student WHERE Name CONTAINING 'eTeR';
```

The Containing keyword instructs Firebird to perform a case-insensitive match search.

In the previous chapter we used LIKE to search for names starting with the letter 'J' or 'j'

… WHERE Name LIKE 'J%' OR Name LIKE 'j%'

Firebird allows us to perform that same search using keywords:
**STARTS, STARTING,** and **STARTING WITH**

The following four SQL statements are valid.

```
SELECT * FROM student WHERE NAME STARTS 'Pe';
SELECT * FROM student WHERE NAME STARTS WITH 'Pe';
SELECT * FROM student WHERE NAME STARTING 'Pe';
SELECT * FROM student WHERE NAME STARTING WITH 'Pe';
```

Another regular expression that Firebird offers that we can use to perform the same search is the **SIMILAR TO,** For example consider the following two examples: Type and execute these examples

```
SELECT * FROM student WHERE NAME SIMILAR TO 'Pe%';
SELECT * FROM student WHERE NAME SIMILAR TO '%e%';
```

You should be presented with similar screens as shown below:

```
SELECT * FROM student WHERE NAME SIMILAR TO 'Pe%';
```

| ABC C | ABC NAME | 123 A | ABC ADDRESS | ABC POST | ABC EMAIL | ABC PHONENO |
|---|---|---|---|---|---|---|
| PH856 | Peter Hollis | 19 | 25 NEW York | NY098365 | p.hollis@abc.com | 0018644774523 |

```
SELECT * FROM student WHERE NAME SIMILAR TO '%e%';
```

SELECT * FROM student WHERE NAME | Enter a SQL expression to filter results (use Ctrl+Space)

| ABC CODE | ABC NAME | 123 A | ABC ADDRESS | ABC POSTZIP | ABC EMAIL | ABC PHONENO |
|---|---|---|---|---|---|---|
| PH856 | Peter Hollis | 19 | 25 NEW York | NY098365 | p.hollis@abc.com | 0018644774523 |
| FL065 | Fiona Jones | 20 | 54 Dyer Avenue | SW98 S76X | fiona.jones@abc.com | 073334554 |
| JH321 | Jane Headly | 21 | 14 Seymore Place | CR54 7YH | jh@def.com | 079854211 |

Both keywords START(ING) etc. and SIMILAR TO are case sensitive.

ⓘ A word of warning. Although these regular expressions are handy and many other RDBMS, have there own equivalent, many of these are specific to a particular RDBMS. Therefore if in the future you wish to port your application to another RDBMS, this may be an up hill challenge, depending on how extensive you employ these regular expressions in your application.

We can also use functions to search text content. We will look at data manipulating functions later on in future chapters. However, to conclude our text search, we take a brief look as the *POSITION* function.

Type and execute the following:

```
SELECT * FROM student WHERE POSITION ('Pe',NAME) > 0;
```

| `SELECT * FROM student WHERE POS` | Enter a SQL expression to filter results (use Ctrl+Space) | | | | | ▼ ⟳ ⍏ |
|---|---|---|---|---|---|---|
| ᴀʙᴄ CO⫯↕? | ᴀʙᴄ NAME↕? | 123⫯↕? | ᴀʙᴄ ADDRESS↕? | ᴀʙᴄ POST⫯↕? | ᴀʙᴄ EMAIL ⫯↕? | ᴀʙᴄ PHONENO |
| PH856 | Peter Hollis | 19 | 25 NEW York | NY098365 | p.hollis@abc.com | 0018644774523 |

The Position function searches for a pattern match text against the column name and returns the position of where the start of the matching text was found. If no match was found then the result would be zero.

Note also that Position is also case sensitive.

[d][i][y] *Things to try...*

1 Modify:
```
SELECT * FROM student WHERE NAME SIMILAR TO '%e%';
```
to be case insensitive.
Hint: using `LOWER` function.

## Summing up chapters 7 to 10

We began chapter 7 with  a more in-depth look at data retrieval. Here we showed how to sort our results with the use of the ***ORDER BY*** instruction. We looked at how the ***WHERE*** clause filtering can be expanded. We further looked at the use of fully qualified table names and their importance when handling more than one table with same column names. We ended this chapter with a brief look at comments and how they aid user readability of SQL scripts.

Chapter 8 was an expansion on the previous chapter but focusing more on  operators such as OR, NULL, NOT, AND and range values and how they can be used in combination.

Finally we concluded with a look at regular expressions in chapter 10 searching text data using keywords such as ***CONTAINING, STARTS, STARTING with and SIMILIAR TO***. We also looked at how the ***POSITION*** Function can be used to perform text search.

# 11  Domains

Domains in Firebird are similar to the concept of 'user-defined data-type'. As you may remember a data-type is basically a way of defining what is the acceptable data that can be held in a column.

Columns (Objects) based on a domain defined will inherit all attributes of that domain, these include such things as data-type, null status, a default value for inserts, etc.

This chapter will introduce you to a few more ideas around working with domains, so read and re-read if necessary, just to get used to any unfamiliar terms.

It is important to note that when you create a domain in the database, you must specify a unique identifier that is global in the database. A common practice amongst developers is to often use a special prefix or suffix in domain identifiers to facilitate self-documentation. For example:

CREATE DOMAIN  D_TYPE_IDENTIFIER...
CREATE DOMAIN  DESCRIPTION_D...

```
CREATE DOMAIN D_POINT AS
NUMERIC(18, 3) [2];
```

One of the merits of domains is that once it has been defined in the database, it can be reused  repeatedly to define table columns, PSQL arguments and PSQL local variables.  It should be noted that some attributes can be overridden when the new object is defined, if required.

Domain syntax is as follows:

```
CREATE DOMAIN domain [AS] <datatype>
[DEFAULT literal |NULL |USER}]
[NOT NULL] [CHECK(<dom_search_condition>)]
[CHARSET charset | NONE}]
[COLLATE collation];
```

Notice, the second paragraph begins 'Columns (Objects)', this is because domain usage is not limited to column definitions for tables and views. Domains can be used to declare input and output parameters and variables in PSQL code.

The benefits of data definition encapsulation become clear if, for example, several tables need columns defined with identical or nearly identical attributes. In other words, once a domain has been defined in the database, it can be reused repeatedly to define table columns, PSQL arguments and PSQL local variables.

In a nutshell, a domain is essentially a data type with optional constraints (restrictions on the allowed set of values).

Domains are also useful for abstracting common constraints on fields into a single location for maintenance. For example, several tables might contain email address columns, all requiring the same CHECK constraint to verify the address syntax. Define a domain rather than setting up each table's constraint individually.

Parameters of a domain...

- *Name* – Unique identifier given to the domain.

- *Data-type* - The underlying data type of the domain. This can include array specifiers.

- *Collation* - An optional collation for the domain. If no collation is specified, the underlying data type's default collation is used. The underlying type must be collatable if **COLLATE** is specified.

- *DEFAULT expression* - DOMAIN can define a default value that the server will use when inserting a new row if the INSERT statement does not include the column in its specification list. Defaults can save time and error during data entry. For example, a possible default for a DATE column could be today's date, or to write the CURRENT_USER context variable into a UserName column.

- *CONSTRAINT constraint_name* - An optional name for a constraint. If not specified, the system generates a name.

- **NOT NULL** - Values of this domain are prevented from being null (but see notes below).

- **NULL** - Values of this domain are allowed to be null. This is the default.

- **CHECK (expression)** - The CHECK constraint provides a wide scope for providing domain attributes that restrict the content of data that can be stored in columns using the domain. The CHECK constraint sets a search condition *(dom_search_condition)* that must be true before data can be accepted into these columns.

Consider the following example:

This example creates the `us_postal_code` data type and then uses the type in a table definition. A regular expression test is used to verify that the value looks like a valid US postal code:

```
CREATE DOMAIN us_postal_code AS VARCHAR(50)
CHECK(
    VALUE ~ '^\d{5}$'
OR VALUE ~ '^\d{5}-\d{4}$'
);

CREATE TABLE us_mail (
    address_id not null constraint pk_usmail primary
key using index ix_id,
    street1 VARCHAR(50) NOT NULL,
    street2 VARCHAR(50),
    street3 VARCHAR(50),
    city VARCHAR(50) NOT NULL,
    postal us_postal_code NOT NULL
);
```

So why would a database developer want to use domains within their organization? Using domains at the database level is a great way of enforcing business rules at this level. That is to say, most database update happens outside the end-user application layer. That is not to say you shouldn't enforce business rules at the application level too, but that the database is the last line of defence, is usually more self-documenting than application code can be, and also protects the database from application programmers.

To demonstrate Domains in action do the following:

```
CREATE DOMAIN dom_code AS VARCHAR(150)
       CHECK (VALUE  LIKE '%@%');


CREATE TABLE student2 (
CODE VARCHAR(20) NOT null primary KEY,
Name VARCHAR(150),
EMAIL dom_code
);
```

```
INSERT INTO student2 (CODE,NAME,EMAIL) VALUES('BHJHG','John
Smith','abcAmymail.com');
```

Now, when you execute the following INSERT statement you should
be presented with the following error message:

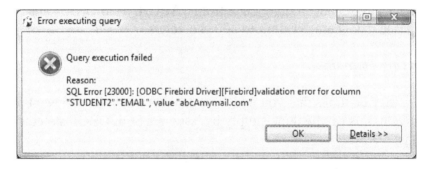

The reason for this is that the column EMAIL is of domain type
dom_code which checks to see if the email contains the '@' character.
In the above insert statement the '@' character is missing in the
emailentry.

Now click the OK button and type and execute the following:

```
INSERT INTO student2 (CODE,NAME,EMAIL) VALUES('BHJHG','John
Smith','abc@mymail.com');
```

replacing the A with @ in the email term for it to read
abc@mymail.com

We can check our entry simply with a SELECT query on table
student2: `SELECT * FROM student2;`

85

Result

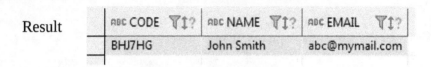

| ᴬᴮᶜ CODE ▽↕? | ᴬᴮᶜ NAME ▽↕? | ᴬᴮᶜ EMAIL ▽↕? |
|---|---|---|
| BHJ7HG | John Smith | abc@mymail.com |

### *Changing an existing Domain...*

In the same way that over time you may wish to alter tables, you may also need to make changes to an existing domain. This can be achieved as follows:

Type and execute the following:

```
ALTER DOMAIN dom_code
   TYPE CHAR(300)
   SET DEFAULT NULL;
```

Here we have changed dom_code from VARCHAR to CHAR and increased that character limit to 300 characters.

### *Deleting Domains...*

There may be times that you no longer require a domain and want to remove it, this can be done simply by issuing a SQL DROP statement, syntax:

```
DROP DOMAIN domain_name
```

For example

```
DROP DOMAIN dom_code;
```

We end this chapter by requesting that you to have a go at the following exercises.

### Things to try...

1/ Create a domain that will check if emails contain '@' AND '.'
2/ Change dom_code back to varchar and reduce character length to 200 characters.

3/ Change Domain dom_code to dom_code2 using the following syntax,

      ALTER DOMAIN <old name> TO <new name>;

test this with a new created table student3 – see student2 for hint.

# 12  Creating Calculated Fields

There are a number of reasons why we may want to use fields that are either formatted to our liking or derived from a calculation. For example:-

- You may wish to calculate a students age from the current date and their date of birth.

- Medical organisations tend to require the data be presented in uppercase.

- Postal systems tend to want the Postal Code to be formatted in a particular way.

- A sales representative may get their travel expense paid based on miles travelled and a standard company rate.

In each of these examples, your application needs the information in a particular way. Now, your application could retrieve the information and then perform the necessary adjustments, but this would not be the most efficient way to do this. The more effective approach is to retrieve converted, calculated, or reformatted data directly from the database.

Calculated fields don't actually exist in database tables. Rather, a calculated field is created on-the-fly within a SQL SELECT statement.

*Fields*. As mentioned in earlier chapters, 'field' and 'column' can be used interchangeably, although database table columns tends to be called 'column', we tend to use the term 'field' if the column was calculated. Thus we use the expression 'calculated field'.

For example suppose we wanted to calculate the approximate year a student was born we could do so as follows:

```
SELECT Name, Age, EXTRACT(YEAR FROM CURRENT_DATE) - AGE
AS YOB FROM student;
```

| ABC NAME | 123 AGE | 123 YOB |
|---|---|---|
| John smith | 19 | 1,999 |
| Peter Hollis | 19 | 1,999 |
| Fiona Jones | 20 | 1,998 |
| Jane Headly | 21 | 1,997 |

In this example we calculated an approximate year of birth (YOB) for our students. However the usual format for a year is not formatted to what we tend to be familiar with. Again we can expand on our calculated field by reformatting the resultant calculation as follows:

```
SELECT Name, Age, LPAD(EXTRACT(YEAR FROM CURRENT_DATE) -
AGE,4) AS YOB FROM student;
```

| ABC NAME | 123 AGE | ABC YOB |
|---|---|---|
| John smith | 19 | 1999 |
| Peter Hollis | 19 | 1999 |
| Fiona Jones | 20 | 1998 |
| Jane Headly | 21 | 1997 |

A brief explanation on the above examples.

To calculate our YOB we first used Firebird's EXTRACT function to extract the year partition on the systems current date we then subtracted the current year from the student age. We then used Firebird's padding function LPAD to format the calculated result to our required format.

(i) Note: in a real live application it would make better sense to record the student's date of birth and have their age calculated as a calculated field.

One final example that we may look at is one that is common. That is, the joining of more that one column to form a single field, this is called concatenation (or concat for short). Different RDBMSs tend to implement this differently. The three most common approaches is either to use the concat function, or the dot operator or as in Firebird's case ||.

For example consider the following;

```
SELECT Name || email AS nameEmail, AGE FROM student;
```

| ᴀʙᴄ NAMEEMAIL | ▽↕? | 123 AGE ▽↕? |
|---|---|---|
| John smith | j.smith@xyz.com | 19 |
| Peter Hollis | p.hollis@abc.com | 19 |
| Fiona Jones | fiona.jones@abc.com | 20 |
| Jane Headly | jh@def.com | 21 |

The example above, forms the nameEmail field by concatenating the Name column with the email column from the student table.

**d l y** *Things to try...*

1/ Display Student names in uppercase.
2/ Join the Student Code with their Name but ensure they are separated with a space.

# 13  Virtual columns

In the previous chapter we discussed calculated fields, where the field does not physically exist but is created during executing an SQL Select statement. That is to say, it is created on-the-fly along with its defined values.

However in this chapter we will be looking at virtual columns.

In relational databases a virtual column is a table column whose value is automatically computed using other columns values, or another deterministic expression. Virtual columns are not part of any SQL standard, and are only implemented by some DBMSs, like MariaDB, SQL Server, Oracle and Firebird.

There are two types of virtual columns:

- Virtual columns;
- Persistent columns.

Virtual columns values are computed *on-the-fly* when needed, for example when they are returned by a SELECT statement. Persistent column values are computed when a row is inserted in a table, and they are written like all other values. They can change if other values change. Both virtual and persistent columns have advantages and disadvantages: virtual columns don't consume space on the disk, but they must be computed every time a query refers to them; persistent columns don't require any CPU time, but they consume disk space. However, sometimes a choice is not available, because some DBMSs support only one column type (or neither of them).

Firebird has always supported virtual columns as its precursor *InterBase* supports it, they're called Computed Columns.

It should be noted that Firebird supports virtual columns, not persistent ones and allows for sub-selects, calling built in functions, external functions and stored routines in the virtual column expression.

**Syntax**

Creating a virtual column can be done during table creation and when adding columns to an existing table, the syntax used to define a virtual column is the following:

```
column_name [type] COMPUTED BY (expression)
```

or the industry standard (SQL-2003-compliant equivalent) which is now supported by Firebird

```
column_name [type] GENERATED ALWAYS AS (expression)
```

As mentioned before Virtual column values are not stored, but are evaluated when rows are read.

It should also be noted that virtual columns are created at table creation.

The following example should aid in our understanding of how we can setup a virtual column.

Consider the following example.

Type and execute the following:

```
CREATE TABLE t1 (
    first_name VARCHAR(10),
    last_name VARCHAR(10),
    full_name VARCHAR(255) GENERATED ALWAYS AS
(first_name || ' ' || last_name)
);
```

In this SQL statement we derive the full_name by concatenation of the first and last name.

Now type and execute the following:

```
INSERT INTO t1 (first_name,last_name)
VALUES('Peter','Brown');
```

Finally type and execute the following:

```
SELECT * FROM t1;
```

You should be presented with the following screen.

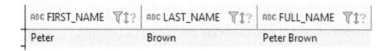

| ABC FIRST_NAME | ABC LAST_NAME | ABC FULL_NAME |
|---|---|---|
| Peter | Brown | Peter Brown |

### Virtual Columns verse Calculated Fields...

Virtual Columns exist at table creation time, whereas calculated fields exist on execution of the SQL SELECT statement.

The value held in the virtual column is calculated by the DBMS when the data is retrieved. The computed column's value does not change until data has been updated and retrieved again.

With calculated fields the value of the Field is calculated in the SQL SELECT statement after the data has been retrieved.

### Things to try...

1/ Create a table and name it 'v*staff*', give it name column, miles column and a virtual column '*exprate*' which has a computed value miles * 5.3. using the Firebird keyword COMPUTED BY

2/ Repeat task 2 but this time use Firebird keyword GENERATED ALWAYS AS.
Insert your own data and check your answers using the select statement.

# Summing up chapters 10 to 13

### *Domains...*
Domains in Firebird are similar to the concept of 'user-defined data-type'. As you may remember data-type is basically a way of defining what are the acceptable data that can be held in a column.

Columns (Objects) based on a domain defined will inherit all attributes of that domain, these include such things as data-type, Null status, a default value for inserts, etc.

Domains are also useful for abstracting common constraints on fields into a single location for maintenance. For example, several tables might contain email address columns, all requiring the same CHECK constraint to verify the address syntax. Define a domain rather than setting up each table's constraint individually.

### *Calculated Fields...*
There are a number of reasons why we may want to use fields that are either formatted to our liking or derived from a calculation. For example, you may wish to calculate a student's age from the current date and their date of birth or a sales representative may get their travel expense paid based on miles traveled and a standard company rate.

Calculated fields don't actually exist in database tables. Rather, a calculated field is created on-the-fly within a SQL SELECT statement.

### *Virtual Columns...*
In relational databases a virtual column is a table column whose value is automatically computed using other columns' values, or another deterministic expression. Virtual columns are not part of any SQL standard, and are only implemented by some DBMSs, like MariaDB, SQL Server, Oracle and Firebird.

Virtual Columns exist at table creation time.
Firebird supports the following syntax for the creation of a virtual column:

```
column_name [type] COMPUTED BY
(expression)
```

and, the industry standard (SQL-2003-compliant equivalent) which is now supported by Firebird.

```
column_name [type] GENERATED ALWAYS AS
(expression)
```

# 14 Firebird Internal Data Manipulation Functions

SQL is no different to any other computer manipulating language, when it comes to functions. Firebird supports the use of functions to manipulate data. In chapters 7 we used the *TRIM* function and in chapter 8 we used the *UPPER* function.

ⓘ It should be noted that functions are DBMS specific and not part of the SQL specification. However Most SQL Implementations support functions. Therefore functions are said to be less portable. Although many of the major RDBMSs aim to include similar interface functions, there are bound to be some that are either specific to the DBMS or simply not included in their implementation.
Therefore some developers aim to keep there use to a minimum. If you find you have to use them, then comment on the code well, so you or others at a later date can make sense of your code.

## *Types of Functions...*

Most SQL implementations support the following types of functions:

- Text manipulation – as mentioned in our previous example text function like **Trim,** for removing head and tail spaces, or converting text from uppercase to lowercase and visa versa using the **Upper and Lower** function.

- Mathematical functions used to carry out mathematical operations on Numeric data for example returning the absolute value of a number using **ABS** function, etc.

- A very useful function you will find in most DBMSs are date and time manipulation functions, where it is used to extract a specific part of the date/time or adding/subtracting dates/time. These are fairly common functions.

- System functions returning DBMS specific information for example, user login, version information, etc.

- Passing data to functions...

Function tend to take the form:

Therefore we pass data to the function eg Result = UPPER(raw data). However because the return data is to the calling parent there is no need for the 'Result =' section. Let us use a few examples to illustrate.

*Text Manipulation functions...*

You have already seen the UPPER and TRIM functions, consider a few more examples.

In the next example we will use the LEFT function to return the left most part of a string of characters.

Type and execute the following:

```
SELECT LEFT(NAME,5) AS NAME FROM student;
```

| ABC NAME |
|----------|
| John     |
| Peter    |
| Fiona    |
| Jane     |

In this example the first 5 characters are returned.

Now suppose we want to return just a portion of the string from anywhere within the entire string of text, in other words we want just the substring of the text, then we can use the **substring** function, for example:

```
SELECT SUBSTRING(NAME FROM 2 FOR 3) FROM student;
```

| ABC SUBSTRING |
|---------------|
| ohn           |
| ete           |
| ion           |
| ane           |

This example returns the substring 3 characters from NAME starting at position 2.

Listed below are commonly used Firebird internal Text Manipulation Functions:

| Function | Description |
|---|---|
| ASCII_CHAR | Returns the ASCII character corresponding to the number passed in the argument. |
| LEFT | Returns the leftmost part of the argument string. |
| LOWER | Returns the lower-case equivalent of the input string. |
| UPPER | Returns the upper-case equivalent of the input string. |
| LPAD | Left-pads a string with spaces or with a user-supplied string until a given length is reached. |
| POSITION | Returns the (1-based) position of the first occurrence of a substring in a host string. |
| REPLACE | Replaces all occurrences of a substring in a string. |
| REVERSE | Returns a string backwards. |
| RIGHT | Returns the rightmost part of the argument string. |
| RPAD | Right-pads a string with spaces or with a user-supplied string until a given length is reached. |
| SUBSTRING | Returns a string's substring starting at the given position, either to the end of the string or with a given length. |
| TRIM | Removes leading and/or trailing spaces (or optionally other strings) from the input string. |
| COALESCE | The function takes two or more arguments and returns the value of the first non-NULL argument. |
| CHAR_LENGTH | Gives the length in characters of the input string. |
| CHARACTER_LENGTH | Gives the length in characters of the input string. |
| HASH | Returns a hash value for the input string. This function fully supports text BLOBs of any length and character set. |

## Date and Time Manipulation functions...

Date and Time functions are one of the most important functions in the Firebird SQL language.

Listed below are commonly used Firebird Date and Time Manipulation Functions

| Function | Description |
|---|---|
| DATEADD | Adds the specified number of years, months, days, hours, minutes, seconds or milliseconds to a date/time value. |
| DATEDIFF | Returns the number of years, months, days, hours, minutes, seconds or milliseconds elapsed between two date/time values. |
| EXTRACT | Extracts and returns an element from a DATE, TIME or |

| | TIMESTAMP expression. |
|---|---|
| CURRENT_DATE | Returns the operating system's current date in the form YYYYMMDD. |
| CURRENT_TIME | Returns the operating system's current time in the form HHMMSS |
| CURRENT_TIMESTAMP | Returns the operating system's current timestamp (date and time) in the form YYYYMMDDHHMMSS. |

Consider the following examples where we simply wish to return the day from the current date.   We simple execute the following examples.

```
SELECT FIRST 1 name, EXTRACT (DAY FROM CURRENT_DATE)
FROM student;
```

| ABC NAME ▼↕? | 123 EXTRACT ▼↕? |
|---|---|
| John smith | 29 |

Returns the day of the current month

```
SELECT FIRST 1 name, EXTRACT (WEEKDAY FROM
CURRENT_DATE) FROM student;
```

Returns Number corresponding to the day of the week where Monday = 1

| ABC NAME ▼↕? | 123 EXTRACT ▼↕? |
|---|---|
| John smith | 4 |

```
SELECT FIRST 1 name, EXTRACT (MONTH FROM CURRENT_DATE)
FROM student;
```

```
SELECT FIRST 1 name, EXTRACT (YEAR FROM CURRENT_DATE)
FROM student;
```

```
SELECT FIRST 1 name, EXTRACT (YEARDAY FROM
CURRENT_DATE) FROM student;
```

```
SELECT FIRST 1 name, EXTRACT (DAY FROM CAST('1976-03-
24' AS DATE)) FROM student;
```

| ABC NAME ▼↕? | 123 EXTRACT ▼↕? |
|---|---|
| John smith | 24 |

By simply using date keywords we can extract the date portion in question.

Now consider the following examples for current date and time.

```
SELECT FIRST 1 name, CURRENT_DATE FROM student;
```

| ABC NAME ⍀↕? | ⏱ CURRENT_DATE ⍀↕? |
|---|---|
| John smith | 2018-03-29 |

```
SELECT FIRST 1 name, CURRENT_TIME FROM student;
```

| ABC NAME ⍀↕? | ⏱ CURRENT_TIME ⍀↕? |
|---|---|
| John smith | 10:56:54 |

```
SELECT FIRST 1 name, CURRENT_TIMESTAMP FROM student;
```

| ABC NAME ⍀↕? | ⏱ CURRENT_TIMESTAMP ⍀↕? |
|---|---|
| John smith | 2018-03-29 10:57:44 |

### Using the DATEADD function...

```
SELECT FIRST 1 name,current_date, DATEADD (13 day to
current_date) FROM student;
```

| ABC NAME ⍀↕? | ⏱ CURRENT_DATE ⍀↕? | ⏱ DATEADD ⍀↕? |
|---|---|---|
| John smith | 2018-03-29 | 2018-04-11 |

```
SELECT FIRST 1 name,current_date, DATEADD (3 MONTH to
current_date) FROM student;
```

| ABC NAME ⍀↕? | ⏱ CURRENT_DATE ⍀↕? | ⏱ DATEADD ⍀↕? |
|---|---|---|
| John smith | 2018-03-29 | 2018-06-29 |

```
SELECT FIRST 1 name,current_date, DATEADD (3 YEAR to
current_date) FROM student;
```

| ABC NAME | CURRENT_DATE | DATEADD |
|---|---|---|
| John smith | 2018-03-29 | 2021-03-29 |

A little explanation is required here, we simply state how many days, months, or years we wish to add to a particular date.

Using the DATEDIFF function.

```
SELECT FIRST 1 name,current_timestamp, DATEDIFF (HOUR FROM
CURRENT_TIMESTAMP TO TIMESTAMP '2018-03-29 13:25') FROM
student;
```

| ABC NAME | CURRENT_TIMESTAMP | 123 DATEDIFF |
|---|---|---|
| John smith | 2018-03-29 11:16:56 | 2 |

```
SELECT FIRST 1 name,current_timestamp, DATEDIFF (MINUTE FROM
TIME '0:00' TO CURRENT_TIME) FROM student;
```

| ABC NAME | CURRENT_TIMESTAMP | 123 DATEDIFF |
|---|---|---|
| John smith | 2018-03-29 11:20:30 | 680 |

```
SELECT FIRST 1 name,current_timestamp, DATEDIFF (MONTH,
CURRENT_DATE, DATE '01-03-2017') FROM student;
```

| ABC NAME | CURRENT_TIMESTAMP | 123 DATEDIFF |
|---|---|---|
| John smith | 2018-03-29 11:34:17 | -14 |

```
SELECT FIRST 1 name,current_timestamp, DATEDIFF (DAY FROM
CURRENT_DATE TO CAST('2019-03-25' AS DATE)) FROM student;
```

| ABC NAME | CURRENT_TIMESTAMP | 123 DATEDIFF |
|---|---|---|
| John smith | 2018-03-29 11:40:00 | 361 |

As you can see the date and time functions are very useful functions. It should be noted that the date and time are stored in tables using special internal formats so they may by sorted or filtered quickly and efficiently, as well as saving physical storage space.

## *Mathematical Manipulation functions...*

Mathematical functions are functions that are used to manipulate numeric data. These functions tend to be used to carry out operations such as algebraic, trigonometric, or geometric calculations.

Listed below are commonly used Firebird Mathematical data Manipulation Functions.

| Function | Description |
|----------|-------------|
| ABS | Returns the absolute value of the argument. |
| ACOS | Returns the arc cosine of the argument. |
| ASIN | Returns the arc sine of the argument. |
| ATAN | Returns the arc tangent of the argument. |
| ATAN2 | Returns the angle whose sine-to-cosine ratio is given by the two arguments, and whose sine and cosine signs correspond to the signs of the arguments. |
| CEIL, CEILING | Returns the smallest whole number greater than or equal to the argument. |
| COS | Returns an angle's cosine. The argument must be given in radians. |
| COSH | Returns the hyperbolic cosine of the argument. |
| COT | Returns an angle's cotangent. The argument must be given in radians. |
| EXP | Returns the natural exponential, $e^{number}$ |
| FLOOR | Returns the largest whole number smaller than or equal to the argument. |
| LN | Returns the natural logarithm of the argument. |
| LOG | Returns the x-based logarithm of y. |
| LOG10 | Returns the 10-based logarithm of the argument. |
| MAXVALUE | Returns the maximum value from a list of numerical, string, or date/time expressions. This function fully supports text BLOBs of any length and character set. |
| MINVALUE | Returns the minimum value from a list of numerical, string, or date/time expressions. This function fully supports text BLOBs of any length and character set. |
| MOD | Returns the remainder of an integer division. |
| PI | Returns an approximation of the value of $\pi$. |
| POWER | Returns x to the y'th power. |

| RAND | Returns a random number between 0 and 1. |
|------|------------------------------------------|
| ROUND | Rounds a number to the nearest integer. |
| SIGN | Returns the sign of the argument: -1, 0 or 1. |
| SIN | Returns an angle's sine. The argument must be given in radians. |
| SINH | Returns the hyperbolic sine of the argument. |
| SQRT | Returns the square root of the argument. |
| TAN | Returns an angle's tangent. The argument must be given in radians. |
| TANH | Returns the hyperbolic tangent of the argument. |

This list shows typical internal functions found in most DBMS functions.

Consider the following:

```
SELECT FIRST 1 name, MOD(6,9) FROM student;
```

| ABC NAME ▼↕? | 123 MOD ▼↕? |
|--------------|-------------|
| John smith | 6 |

```
SELECT FIRST 1 name, MOD(9,6) FROM student;
```

| ABC NAME ▼↕? | 123 MOD ▼↕? |
|--------------|-------------|
| John smith | 3 |

```
SELECT FIRST 1 name, (3-7), ABS(3-7)  FROM student;
```

| ABC NAME ▼↕? | 123 SUBTRACT ▼↕? | 123 ABS ▼↕? |
|--------------|------------------|-------------|
| John smith | -4 | 4 |

***Boolean Logic Manipulatiion functions...***

Firebird supports basic boolean operations.

A boolean function is a mathematical function that maps arguments to a value, where the allowable values of a range (the function arguments) and domain (the function value) are just one of two values: true and false (or 0 and 1).

Listed below are commonly used Firebird Boolean data Manipulation Functions.

| Function | Description |
|----------|-------------|
| BIN_AND | Returns the result of the bitwise AND operation on the argument(s). |
| BIN_OR | Returns the result of the bitwise OR operation on the argument(s). |
| BIN_SHL | Returns the first argument bitwise left-shifted by the second argument, i.e. a << b or a·2^b. |
| BIN_SHR | Returns the first argument bitwise right-shifted by the second argument, i.e. a >> b or a/2^b. |
| BIN_XOR | Returns the result of the bitwise XOR operation on the argument(s). |

Consider the following examples:

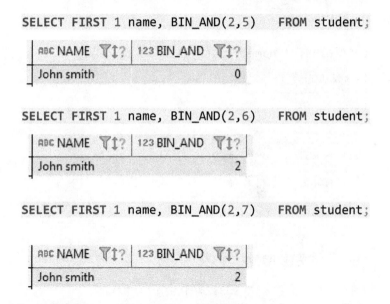

```
SELECT FIRST 1 name, BIN_AND(2,5)    FROM student;
```

| ABC NAME | 123 BIN_AND |
|----------|-------------|
| John smith | 0 |

```
SELECT FIRST 1 name, BIN_AND(2,6)    FROM student;
```

| ABC NAME | 123 BIN_AND |
|----------|-------------|
| John smith | 2 |

```
SELECT FIRST 1 name, BIN_AND(2,7)    FROM student;
```

| ABC NAME | 123 BIN_AND |
|----------|-------------|
| John smith | 2 |

The above examples may be a bit confusing at first, but try to remember back to your schooldays and maths lessons on boolean algebra: The table below shows binary representations of the numbers 0 to 7 (rows) based on the 'bit' weighting (columns).

| 4 | 2 | 1 | |
|---|---|---|---|
| 0 | 0 | 0 | 0 |
| 0 | 0 | 0 | 1 |
| 0 | 1 | 0 | 2 |
| 0 | 1 | 1 | 3 |
| 1 | 0 | 0 | 4 |
| 1 | 0 | 1 | 5 |
| 1 | 1 | 0 | 6 |
| 1 | 1 | 1 | 7 |

The table shows binary representations of the numbers 0 to 7 and their bit weighting.

Therefore if we wanted to represent the number 3 in binary we say there is 1 bit in the two column plus 1 bit in the one column, therefore 2+1 = 3.

Now the AND operation will return a true if both arguments are true. Therefore if we ADD 0,1,0  with

1,1,0

Then only column 2 is equal (true) therefore we would get 2 for rows 2,3,6,7.

### A note on Firebird's External Functions (User Define Function 'UDF')...

In this chapter so far we have focused on commonly used internal functions, the list is by no means complete and as Firebird is under continuous development we can expect additional functionalities in the future.

However, it is more than likely that you will come across a need for a function that does not come shipped with Firebird function you need. Firebird also supports User Define Function (UDF) also known as external functions.

External functions, are programs written in an external programming language and stored in dynamically loaded libraries. Once declared to a database, they become available in dynamic and procedural statements as though they were implemented in the SQL language internally.

External functions extend the possibilities for processing data with SQL considerably. To make a function available to a database, it is declared using the statement DECLARE EXTERNAL FUNCTION.

The library containing a function is loaded when any function included in it is called.

However as these are not portable, we will not be covering this topic within this book.

Readers wishing further information can visit:

https://firebirdsql.org/file/documentation/reference_manuals/fblangref25-en/html/fblangref25-ddl-extfunc.html

ⓘ It should be noted that future Firebird versions will be aiming to remove UDF, due to various security issues. It is therefore recommended that you either replace UDF with UDR or stored functions. You will be please to know that many of the UDF became built-in functions in version 4.0

1/ Using the RIGHT function, write a SELECT statement to return the first 3 characters from the NAME column from the STUDENT table.

2/ Type and execute some of the Date and Time functions presented in this chapter.

3/ Type and execute some of the Boolean functions presented in this chapter.

4/ Use the RAND to return random numbers between _**0 and 100,**_ whole numbers only.

Hint place one function within another. That is the output of one function becomes the input to another.

# 15  Summarising Data

*Firebird Aggregate Functions...*

So far we have focused on individual records, or simply listings. However it is often necessary to summarize some or all our data without retrieving it all. Firebird provides functions for that purpose. By using these functions we can retrieve data for analysis purposes. We can produce reports too, for example:

- Retrieve the number of rows in a table.
- Obtain the sum of a group of rows in a table
- Find the Maximum, Minimum or Average value in a table column.

Firebird aggregate function are:

| Function | Description |
|----------|-------------|
| AVG | AVG returns the average argument value in the group. NULL is ignored. |
| COUNT | COUNT returns the number of non-null values in a group. |
| LIST | LIST returns a string consisting of the non-NULL argument values in the group, separated either by a comma or by a user-supplied separator. If there are no non-NULL values (this includes the case where the group is empty), NULL is returned. |
| MAX | MAX returns the maximum non-NULL element in the result set. |
| MIN | MIN returns the maximum non-NULL element in the result set. |
| SUM | SUM calculates and returns the sum of non-null values in the group. |

In this chapter we will take a brief look at each one of these functions.

ⓘ Aggregate functions operate on groups of records, rather than on individual records or variables. They are often used in combination with a GROUP BY clause. We will be looking at the GROUP BY clause in the next chapter, for now just use it in the exercises.

Before we can demonstrate the aggregate functions we need to amend our student table example.

Let us add a gender column to our student table using the ALTER command.

```
ALTER TABLE STUDENT ADD GENDER VARCHAR(100) DEFAULT
NULL;
```

Now update our student table. Type and execute the following:

```
UPDATE STUDENT SET GENDER='Male' WHERE Age = 19;
```

```
UPDATE STUDENT SET GENDER='Female' WHERE Age <> 19;
```

Now check your updates by typing and executing the following:

```
SELECT NAME, AGE, GENDER FROM student;
```

You get the following:

| ABC NAME | 123 AGE | ABC GENDER |
|----------|---------|------------|
| John smith | 19 | Male |
| Peter Hollis | 19 | Male |
| Fiona Jones | 20 | Female |
| Jane Headly | 21 | Female |

*AVG Function...*

Let us begin with the AVG function. The AVG() function returns the average value of a numeric column.

We can use it to average a group or the whole table column.

Consider the following:

```
SELECT AVG(AGE) FROM student;
```

| 123 AVG |
|---------|
| 19 |

Here we found the average age of our students as a whole.

109

Consider our next example:

```
SELECT GENDER,AVG(AGE) FROM student GROUP BY GENDER;
```

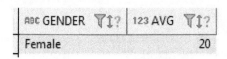

Here we found the average age for Female and Male students.

```
SELECT GENDER,AVG(AGE) FROM student GROUP BY GENDER HAVING
GENDER='Female';
```

Here we only wanted information on female students. Note we replace the WHERE clause with the HAVING clause. We will explore this in
Later chapters. HAVING is usually found with aggregate functions.

In these examples we used the AVG function to find average ages of students either as a whole or a group by gender and applying the HAVING clause filter.

*Count Function…*

The COUNT returns the number of non-null values in a group.

In other words, The COUNT() function returns the number of rows that matched a specified criteria.

Consider the following where we want to know how many records exist in our student table:

```
SELECT COUNT(*) AS ct FROM student;
```

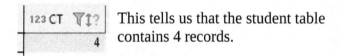

This tells us that the student table contains 4 records.

Now consider the following where we want to count the number of students by their age grouping:

```
SELECT AGE, COUNT(*) AS ct FROM student GROUP BY AGE;
```

| 123 AGE | 123 CT |
|---|---|
| 19 | 2 |
| 20 | 1 |
| 21 | 1 |

This example says that there are two students that are aged 19, one aged 20 and one aged 21.

*LIST Function...*

LIST returns a string consisting of the non-NULL argument values in the group, separated either by a comma or by a user-supplied separator. If there are no non-NULL values (this includes the case where the group is empty), NULL is returned.

Consider the following example:

```
SELECT LIST (NAME, ';') FROM student;
```

| LIST |
|---|
| John smith  ;Peter Hollis  ;Fiona Jones  ;Jane Headly |

Returns a delimited list of Name for every row in the student table.

Now consider our next example:

```
SELECT AGE, LIST (NAME, ';') FROM student GROUP BY AGE;
```

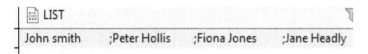

| 123 AGE | LIST |
|---|---|
| 19 | John smith  ;Peter Hollis |
| 20 | Fiona Jones |
| 21 | Jane Headly |

We have a separate list depending on their age.

111

## MAX Function...

The Max function returns the highest value in a specified column. If the argument is a string, this is the value that comes last when the active collation is applied.

Consider the following example where we want to know what is the oldest aged student we have.

```
SELECT max(age) AS oldest FROM student;
```

| 123 OLDEST ⊽↕? |
| --- |
| 21 |

Consider our next example where we wish to know what age is the oldest Male and Female students we have.

```
SELECT gender, max(age) AS oldest FROM student GROUP BY gender;
```

| ᴀʙᴄ GENDER ⊽↕? | 123 OLDEST ⊽↕? |
| --- | --- |
| Female | 21 |
| Male | 19 |

## MAXVALUE Function...

Firebird supports MAXVALUE. Returns the maximum value from a list of numerical, string, or date/time expressions. This function fully supports text BLOBs of any length and character set.

Consider the following example:

```
SELECT (MAXVALUE(5,2,5,7,1,6,2)) AS HighestNo FROM student;
```

| 123 HIGHESTNO ⊽↕? |
| --- |
| 7 |
| 7 |
| 7 |
| 7 |

This example finds the maxvalue in the list but outputs the result for every record in the table. What we want is to only have one record return. We could use the *FIRST 1* LIMIT clause we introduced in previous chapters. Or we could use MAX with MAXVALUE.

## MAX Function using MAXVALUE...

We can use max with maxvalue to get a single record for the largest value.

Consider the following example where we want to find the highest number from a list of the *'HighestNo'*.

```
SELECT MAX(MAXVALUE(5,2,5,7,1,6,2)) AS HighestNo FROM
student;
```

| 123 HIGHESTNO ▼↕? |
|---|
| 7 |

## FIRST With MAXVALUE...

It should be noted that using FIRST in this case example has a slight performance advantage over Max with Maxvalue.

```
SELECT FIRST 1 (MAXVALUE(5,2,5,7,1,6,2)) AS HighestNo
FROM student;
```

| 123 HIGHESTNO ▼↕? |
|---|
| 7 |

## MIN Function...

The Min function returns the smallest value in a specified column. If the argument is a string, this is the value that comes last when the active collation is applied.

Consider the following example where we want to know what the youngest aged students we have.

```
SELECT MIN(age) AS youngest FROM student;
```

| 123 YOUNGEST ▼↕? |
|---|
| 19 |

Consider our next example where we wish to know what age is the youngest Male and Female students we have.

```
SELECT gender, MIN(age) AS youngest FROM student GROUP
BY gender;
```

| ᴬᴮᶜ GENDER ▽↕? | 123 YOUNGEST ▽↕? |
|---|---|
| Female | 20 |
| Male | 19 |

## MINVALUE Function...

Firebird supports MINVALUE. It returns the minimum value from a list of numerical, string, or date/time expressions. This function fully supports text BLOBs of any length and character set.

Consider the following example:

```
SELECT (MINVALUE(5,2,5,7,1,6,2)) AS Lowest FROM
student;
```

| 123 LOWEST ▽↕? |
|---|
| 1 |
| 1 |
| 1 |
| 1 |

This example finds the minvalue in the list but outputs the result for every record in the table. What we want is to only have one record returned. We could use the **FIRST 1** Limit clause we introduced in previous chapters. Or we could use Min with Minvalue.

## MIN Function using MINVALUE...

We can use min with minvalue to get a single record for the smallest value.

Consider the following example where we want to find the smallest number from a list of the smallest 'number'.

```
SELECT MIN(MINVALUE(5,2,5,7,1,6,2)) AS Lowest FROM
student;
```

| 123 LOWEST ▽↕? |
|---|
| 1 |

114

### FIRST With MINVALUE...

As stated previously using FIRST with MINVALUE the same applies here, that using FIRST in this case example has a slight performance advantage over Min with Minvalue.

```
SELECT FIRST 1 (MINVALUE(5,2,5,7,1,6,2)) AS Lowest FROM
student;
```

| 123 LOWEST |
|---|
| 1 |

### SUM Function...

Our final aggregate function we will look at, is the SUM function. The SUM function calculates and returns the sum of non-null values in the group.

Not that you ever would, but consider the following example, where you want to know the sum age of all the students, and how many students that it represents.

```
SELECT count(*) AS No_Of_Students, SUM(age) AS
Total_Age FROM student;
```

| 123 NO_OF_STUDENTS | 123 TOTAL_AGE |
|---|---|
| 4 | 79 |

Now previously we used the AVG function to calculate the average student age. We can now perform the same operation using both the SUM and COUNT aggregate functions, as shown below.

```
SELECT count(*) AS No_Of_Students, SUM(age) / count(*)
AS Average_Age FROM student;
```

| 123 NO_OF_STUDENTS | 123 AVERAGE_AGE |
|---|---|
| 4 | 19 |

In this example we combined two aggregates to obtain a meaningful result.

We can further expand our SQL query to group by gender as shown below:

```
SELECT Gender, count(*) AS No_Of_Students, SUM(age) /
count(*) AS Average_Age FROM student GROUP BY gender;
```

| ᴀʙᴄ GENDER ⵖ‼? | 123 NO_OF_STUDENTS ⵖ‼? | 123 AVERAGE_AGE ⵖ‼? |
|---|---|---|
| Female | 2 | 20 |
| Male | 2 | 19 |

⌨ *Things to try...*

1/ For each of the aggregate functions retype and expand on the examples. Try and guess what the output would be before executing your SQL statements. Execute them to check your answers.

2/ Using a combination of aggregate functions calculate the age difference between the maximum and minimum student.

# 16  Grouping Data

In the last chapter we looked at aggregating functions. In using aggregate functions we briefly touched on grouping. In this chapter we will look into grouping data in more detail.

Many of the calculations thus far were performed on all the data in the table or on matching criteria using the WHERE clause, with the exception of a few we used grouping without any explanation as to why we used the GROUP BY statement.

In one of our previous examples we wanted to find the oldest students based on gender. This is where the role of groups play their part. As shown in the example below.

```
SELECT gender, max(age) AS oldest FROM student GROUP BY
gender;
```

| ABC GENDER ▼↕? | 123 OLDEST ▼↕? |
|----------------|----------------|
| Female         | 21             |
| Male           | 19             |

### Creating Groups...

Groups are created using the **GROUP BY** clause in a SELECT statement.

Consider the following example where you may wish to know the age range of students you currently have.

```
SELECT age FROM student GROUP BY age;
```

| 123 AGE ▼↕? |
|-------------|
| 19          |
| 20          |
| 21          |

In this example the **SELECT** statement specifies a single column, *age*, from the student table. The **GROUP BY** clause instructs Firebird to

117

sort the data and group it by *age*. By grouping in this way this give a single occurrence of each group (in this case *age*).

Now consider our next example, here we may want to know from the grouping of student's age how many are aged 19, how many are 20, etc. By using the GROUP BY clause we can get our results as follows:

```
SELECT age, count (*) AS NumOf FROM student GROUP BY
age;
```

| 123 AGE ▽↕? | 123 NUMOF ▽↕? |
|---|---|
| 19 | 2 |
| 20 | 1 |
| 21 | 1 |

In the example above the **SELECT** statement specifies two columns, age, which contains the student *age* and *NumOf*, which is a calculated field (created by the **COUNT**(*) function). The **GROUP BY** clause instructs Firebird to sort the data and group it by *age*. This causes *NumOf* to be calculated once per age group, rather than once for the entire table.

As you can see from this example there are two students that are aged 19 and two that are aged 20 and 21.  Because we used **GROUP BY**, we did not have to specify each group to be evaluated and calculated. That was done automatically. The **GROUP BY** clause instructs Firebird to group the data and then perform the calculation on each group rather than on the entire resultant set.

There are a number of important rules to remember when using the **GROUP BY** clause:

- By using the **GROUP BY** clause, you can add more than one column to the group, enabling you to nest groups, which is very useful for reporting.  This provides you with granular control over how your data is grouped.

- By nesting groups in your **GROUP BY** clause, the data at the last specified group, is the one that is summarized.

118

- Every column listed in the **GROUP BY** clause must be present in the **SELECT** statement.

- If the grouping column contains a NULL value in one of the rows then the returned group will be NULL. This includes multiple rows with NULL values.

- The **GROUP BY** clause must come after any **WHERE** clause and before any **ORDER BY** clause.

### *Filtering Groups...*

In earlier chapters we were able to filter our data using the **WHERE** clause. However the **WHERE** clause does not work with **GROUP BY**. Firebird still allows us to filter our **GROUP BY** clause with the use of the **HAVING** clause. It should be noted that **HAVING** supports all of **WHERE's** operators.

Consider the following example:

```
SELECT GENDER,AVG(AGE) FROM student GROUP BY GENDER
HAVING GENDER='Female';
```

Here we only wanted information on female students. Note: we replace the *WHERE* clause with the **HAVING** clause. We will explore this in Later chapters. **HAVING** is usually found with aggregate functions.

So what is the difference between using **WHERE** and **HAVING?** Well, the main difference is that **WHERE** filters before the data is grouped where **HAVING** filters after the data is grouped.

Using **WHERE** and **HAVING** together...

There are times when you may need to use both **WHERE** and **HAVING** together. Consider the following example:

```
SELECT age, count (*) AS NumOf
FROM student
```

```
WHERE gender='Female'
GROUP BY age
HAVING count(*) = 1;
```

| 123 AGE ▽⌑? | 123 NUMOF ▽⌑? |
|---|---|
| 20 | 1 |
| 21 | 1 |

The **WHERE** clause can include a column that is not included in the **SELECT** statement.

In the above example the first two lines are our basic SELECT statement. The **WHERE** clause filters all rows where the student gender is females. The data are *then* grouped by age using the **GROUP BY** clause. These groups are now filtered using the **HAVING** clause to return rows where the count is one.

### GROUPING and SORTING...

Earlier we said that grouping sorts the data then groups them. However we must distinguish the difference between grouping and sorting.

If you remember, we sort our data by using the **ORDER BY** clause and **DESC** or **ASC** to say in which direction.

**ORDER BY** sorts the data and generates the results. You can use any column to sort by. It is not mandatory that you include an ORDER BY in your statement, but without it you can not rely on the order of the results.

**GROUP BY** groups that data but the order of the group maybe in any order, and again you can not rely on the order. Therefore it is common practice to use the **ORDER BY** clause to order your results, even if the result appears to be in the order you want, it should not be relied on that it will be in the required order without stating the intended ordering.

Consider the following example:

```
SELECT GENDER, AVG(AGE), count(*) NumOf FROM student
GROUP BY GENDER, age;
```

| ABC GENDER ▼↕? | 123 AVG ▼↕? | 123 NUMOF ▼↕? |
| --- | --- | --- |
| Female | 20 | 1 |
| Female | 21 | 1 |
| Male | 19 | 2 |

In the above example we grouped first by gender and then age. Now the result appears to be in the intended order but this cannot be relied on. A better SQL statement would be as follows:

```
SELECT GENDER, AVG(AGE), count(*) AS NumOf
FROM student
GROUP BY
GENDER, age
ORDER BY gender, age;
```

This would give the intended result.

To further demonstrate this, let us add another student to the student table. Type and execute the following:

```
INSERT INTO Student
(CODE,NAME,AGE,ADDRESS,POSTZIP,EMAIL,PHONENO,GENDER,DOB)
VALUES ('DFRE3W','Mathew Syed',18,'12 Victoria Park, Cedar Sq,
Milton Keynes','MK23
4RF','msyed@mymail.com','0198344735','Male','2000-06-25');
```

Now we may wish to still group our list by gender followed by age, but we may also wish to have the age sorted differently, for example:

```
SELECT GENDER, AVG(AGE), count(*)
NumOf
FROM student
GROUP BY GENDER, age
ORDER BY gender ASC, age DESC;
```

| ABC GENDER ▼↕? | 123 AVG ▼↕? | 123 NUMOF ▼↕? |
| --- | --- | --- |
| Female | 21 | 1 |
| Female | 20 | 1 |
| Male | 19 | 2 |
| Male | 18 | 1 |

In this example we want to have the Age occurrence in descending order.

In closing there are a few handy tips that are worth mentioning when using the group by clause.

- When using the group by clause it is good practice to state the intended ordering that you want.

- Another main difference between ORDER BY and GROUP BY is that the ORDER BY sort will display all the data in the table (within your criteria), where as the GROUP BY reduces similar values to one record.

- Using the WHERE clause with grouping, reduces the amount of data to group. WHERE always comes before GROUP BY.

- The WHERE clause evaluates data before the GROUP BY clause does. When you want to limit data after it's grouped, use HAVING.

- Grouping data can help you analyse your data, but sometimes you'll need a bit more information than just the groups themselves. You can add an aggregate function to summarize grouped data.

Finally, we can take a closing look at the SELECT clause and its sequences.

The SQL statement will start with the SELECT clause, specifying the columns and/or expression, this will be followed by the FROM clause stating the table(s) to retrieve data from. The WHERE clause would only be needed if row-level filtering is required.

The GROUP BY will be used if you need to calculate aggregates by group.
You can use the HAVING clause for group level-filtering, if you wish to limit the results.

ORDER BY is not required but recommended to sort your results. Use the LIMIT clause if you want to limit the number of records retrieved. In other words we have the following sequence:

*SELECT*
*FROM*

*WHERE*
*GROUP BY*
*HAVING*
*ORDER BY*
*LIMIT*

# 17 Working with Sub-queries

Up to this point, all the SELECT queries have been simple queries, retrieving data from a single table within our database.

However SQL also allows us to create sub-queries (also known as inner queries or nested queries).
Sub-queries allow us the ability to perform operations in multiple steps. For example, if you wanted to take the sums of several columns, then average all of those values, you'd need to do each aggregation in a distinct step.

### Understanding the Basics...

Sub-queries can be used in several places within our main query. Let us start with a simple example.

Consider the following example:

```
SELECT sub.*
      FROM
      (
      SELECT *
      FROM student
      WHERE gender='Male'
) Sub
WHERE sub.age =19;
```

| ᴀʙᴄ CODE ▼↕? | ᴀʙᴄ NAME ▼↕? | 123 AGE ▼↕? | ᴀʙᴄ ADDRESS |
|---|---|---|---|
| SK765 | John smith | 19 | 123456 Pitts Avenu |
| PH856 | Peter Hollis | 19 | 25 NEW York |

Let us take a closer look at what is happening.

The **basic rule** when working with sub-queries is to always start with the deepest nested query and work outwards.

Therefore, we start with the inner most query:

```
SELECT *
FROM student
WHERE gender='Male'
```

If we were to run this query we would get a list of all our Male students listing the complete columns.

Although this example may seem obvious to you, the important thing here to take into account is that Firebird (and all other RDBMSs), will treat each SELECT query block as independent queries. Once the inner query block has run, then the next outer block is ran using the results from the inner block as its underlying table (resultant record set).

This leaves us with:

```
SELECT sub.*
       FROM
       (
       <Result from inner query>
       ) Sub
WHERE sub.age =19;
```

Note that the columns used in the inner query can be seen by the outer query.

This example could have been constructed in a single stage query using the **WHERE** clause to perform the filtering on *age* and *gender*.

In previous chapters you may have noticed that the SQL statements were mainly written in a single line. However in some cases they were constructed over multiple lines: this was simply for clarity in reading.

As your queries become more complex it is recommended that you construct your queries in such a way that it allows yourself and others to clearly understand what the query is intended to perform. If the above sub-query was written on a single line, it would be quite challenging, especially for a beginner to understand the query. Therefore, always keep in mind that someone else may have to maintain your code once you have moved on to greener pastures.

*Using sub-queries to aggregate in multiple stages...*

The following example is used to simply demonstrate how you can use sub-queries to aggregate in multiple stages, as shown below:

```
SELECT sub.GENDER, sub.CalAGE, count(sub.ct) SameAge,
sub.x
FROM
(
   SELECT  GENDER,dob, EXTRACT (YEAR FROM CURRENT_DATE)
 - EXTRACT (YEAR FROM
   CAST(DOB AS DATE)) AS CalAGE, 1 AS ct, count(*) AS x
   FROM student
   GROUP BY dob, gender
) sub
GROUP BY sub.GENDER, sub.CalAGE, sub.ct, sub.x
```

| ᴬᴮᶜ GENDER ▼ℤ? | 123 CALAGE ▼ℤ? | 123 SAMEAGE ▼ℤ? | 123 X ▼ℤ? |
|---|---|---|---|
| Female | 20 | 1 | 1 |
| Female | 21 | 1 | 1 |
| Male | 18 | 1 | 1 |
| Male | 19 | 2 | 1 |

It should be noted that our simple CalAGE calculation is an approximate age. We will address how to calculate age from date of birth shortly.

*Sub-queries in conditional logic...*

In chapter 9 we looked at a simple example of using the IN operator. We can also use the IN clause to look for matches in another table. Using the substudent table you created in our earlier chapters, we can perform the following:

```
SELECT code,name, dob
FROM student
WHERE code IN
(
      SELECT code
      FROM substudent
      ORDER BY code
)
```

| ᴬᴮᶜ CODE ▼ℤ? | ᴬᴮᶜ NAME ▼ℤ? | 🕔 DOB ▼ℤ? |
|---|---|---|
| SK765 | John smith | 1999-03-02 |
| PH856 | Peter Hollis | 1999-01-25 |

In the example we look in both the STUDENT and SUBSTUDENT tables for matching CODE in the code column.

One benefit of using the IN clause is that is allows us to build highly dynamic WHERE clause sub-queries.

ⓘ Note that the ORDER BY, in the inner query, has no effect on the final result. You can check this by adding ASC or DESC to the end. To order the result you will need to apply the ORDER BY at the final stage when using the **IN** clause.

*Joining subqueries...*

We can join sub-queries to give the exact same results as using the JOIN clause. Consider the following example:

```
SELECT substudent.code, substudent.name,substudent.dob
FROM student substudent
JOIN (
        SELECT code
        FROM substudent
        ORDER BY code
) sub
ON substudent.code = sub.code
```

| | ABɕ CODE ▽ɪ? | ABC NAME ▽ɪ? | ◷ DOB ▽ɪ? |
|---|---|---|---|
| 1 | PH856 | Peter Hollis | 1999-01-25 |
| 2 | SK765 | John smith | 1999-03-02 |

We will return to the JOIN operations in future chapters when we look at joining tables.

ⓘ Note that the ORDER BY in this example does order the results. You can check this by adding ASC or DESC to the end.

*Select with IIF statement...*

The IIF function usually referred to as a logical function. IIF() takes three arguments. If the first evaluates to 'true', then the second argument is returned; otherwise the third is returned.
We can consider the IIF() as the shorthand way of writing IF Else, and CASE statements. This function will accept three arguments: first

argument is the Boolean expression (which returns true or false) - if the expression result is TRUE then the second argument will be returned as the result otherwise, the third argument will be returned as output.

Let us see the syntax of the Firebird IIF function:

```
IIF (<condition>, ResultT, ResultF)
```

Consider the following example.

```
SELECT name, dob, ROUND(TRUNC(age,0)) AS age
FROM
(
   SELECT name, dob, IIF(leapyear=0, datediff(day,
      dob,CURRENT_DATE) / 365.22,datediff(day,
      dob,CURRENT_DATE) / 365.20) AS age
FROM
      (
         SELECT name, dob, MOD(EXTRACT (YEAR FROM
            CURRENT_DATE),4) AS leapyear
         FROM student
      ) sub
) subsub;
```

| ABC NAME | DOB | 123 AGE |
|---|---|---|
| John smith | 1999-03-02 | 19 |
| Peter Hollis | 1999-01-25 | 19 |
| Mathew Syed | 2000-06-25 | 17 |
| Fiona Jones | 1998-09-28 | 19 |
| Jane Headly | 1997-11-14 | 20 |

In the above example we use multiple sub-queries to calculate the actual age of the student based on their day of birth. However to get an accurate age we need to determine if the year is a leap year or not, in this case we used the IIF logical function.

Let us take a closer look at this example. Remember that we must always start from the inner most query. We first determined if the current year is a leap year.

```
SELECT name, dob, MOD(EXTRACT (YEAR FROM CURRENT_DATE),4) AS
leapyear FROM student
```

We then take the results from this query and pass it up to the next
query, i.e.

```
        SELECT name, dob, IIF(leapyear=0, datediff(day,
        dob,CURRENT_DATE) /
              365.22,datediff(day, dob,CURRENT_DATE) /
        365.20) AS age
        FROM
             (
             <Result from inner query>
             ) sub
```

By using the leapyear field result, we can instruct Firebird of our
decision as to which conditional statement we want executed. Now, the
age result will be in a decimal format, but we are only interested in the
integer portion on the number. Therefore we again needed to pass the
results from this query up the chain to another query to handle the
correct presentation of the number.

```
    SELECT name,dob, ROUND(TRUNC(age,0)) AS age
    FROM
    (
         ... . . .


    )
```

It should be noted that if we simply casted the age as an INT, this will
simply round the age value up. We must first zero out the decimal
portion of the number then we can ROUND the number to an integer
value.

### Select with *CASE* statement...

The CASE statement is SQL's way of handling if/then logic. The
CASE statement is followed by at least one pair of WHEN and THEN
statements. Therefore we could have written the above example using
the CASE logical function instead of IIF.

Consider the following example:

```
SELECT name,dob, ROUND(TRUNC(age,0)) AS age
```

```
FROM
(
SELECT name, dob,
CASE
        WHEN leapyear = 0 THEN datediff(day,
          dob,CURRENT_DATE) / 365.22
        ELSE datediff(day, dob,CURRENT_DATE) / 365.20
END AS age
FROM
(
SELECT name, dob,MOD(EXTRACT (YEAR FROM
   CURRENT_DATE),4) AS leapyear
FROM student
) AS sub
) subsub;
```

| ABC NAME | DOB | 123 AGE |
|----------|-----|---------|
| John smith | 1999-03-02 | 19 |
| Peter Hollis | 1999-01-25 | 19 |
| Mathew Syed | 2000-06-25 | 17 |
| Fiona Jones | 1998-09-28 | 19 |
| Jane Headly | 1997-11-14 | 20 |

The explanation for the example would be the same as previously for the IIF function, with the exception that the CASE function handles the switching condition.

Every CASE statement must end with the END statement. The ELSE statement is optional, and provides a way to capture values not specified in the WHEN/THEN statements.

In this example the CASE work in the following way.

The CASE uses the leapyear value to determine which statement to execute, it repeats this for each row in the resultant query.

### Adding multiple conditions to a CASE statement...

We can also define a number of outcomes in a *CASE* statement by including as many *WHEN/THEN* statements we need, consider the following: (Please note at the time of writing this DBeaver ODBC driver have not fully implemented the CASE statement using strings, therefore this example will be shown via isql command-line interface we introduced in earlier chapters). *(Remember to close DBeaver)*

Consider the following as an example of adding multiple conditions to the CASE statement.

```
SQL> select name, age, code,
CON>        CASE
CON>            WHEN TRIM(upper((gender))) = 'MALE' THEN 'M'
CON>            WHEN TRIM(upper((gender))) = 'FEMALE' THEN 'F'
CON>            ELSE 'Unknown'
CON>        END SEX
CON> FROM student;
```

Result

| NAME | AGE | CODE | SEX |
|------|-----|------|-----|
| John smith | 19 | SK765 | M |
| Peter Hollis | 19 | PH856 | M |
| Mathew Syed | 18 | DFRE3W | M |
| Fiona Jones | 20 | BHJHG | F |
| Jane Headly | 21 | JH321 | F |

*IIF vs CASE...*

One major advantage the CASE statement have over the IIF in the above example would be if we wanted to implement multiple conditions using the IIF function we would need to nest IIF within IIF to get a single return result. If there were a long list this could be quite confusing.

Another advantage of using the CASE statement is that with the CASE statement once the condition is met and the result is returned, there is no need to continue down the list to check future conditions.

If there is only, say, two possible outcomes then the IIF statement maybe preferable. However, CASE is portable across most DBMS where IIF is not as portable.

For this reason it is recommended you use CASE statement over IIF statement.

CASE statements are considered able to execute slightly faster than IIF statement, but this does depend on a number of criteria.

# 18  Joining Tables

One of the main powerful features of relational databases is in how simple it is in joining multiple tables in one query statement on-the-fly. All the techniques we have learned so far, can be applied to Joined tables.

SELECT SQL joins are one of the most important operations you can perform in the SQL grammar, therefore a good understanding of joins and join syntax is an extremely important part of learning SQL.

We have covered briefly the introduction to the relational database model. We now need to put this into practice and see how SQL and Firebird implement the SQL specification.

Before we begin we need to add more tables to our database.

If we continue with our student in our university. We need to record the course he/she is currently taking. Let us recap our scenario:

So far our student table now has the following columns:

## Student Table

| CODE | NAME | AGE | ADDRESS | POSTZIP | EMAIL | PHONENO | GENDER | DOB |
|---|---|---|---|---|---|---|---|---|
| SK765 | John smith | 19 | 123456 Pitts Avenue | IO98 76X | j.smith@xyz.com | 071234566 | Male | 1999-03-02 |
| PH856 | Peter Hollis | 19 | 25 NEW York | NY098365 | p.hollis@abc.co m | 0018644774523 | Male | 1999-01-25 |
| DFRE3W | Mathew Syed | 18 | 12 Victoria Park, Cedar Sq. Milton Keynes | MK23 4RF | fiona.jones@abc. com | 0198344735 | Male | 2000-06-25 |
| BHJHG | Fiona Jones | 20 | 54 Dyer Avenue | SW98 S76X | Jane Headly | 073334554 | Female | 1998-09-28 |
| JH321 | Jane Headly | 21 | 14 Seymore Place | CR54 7YH | jh@def.com | 079854211 | Female | 1997-11-14 |

CODE is our primary key, a unique information that identifies the row. It should be noted that primary keys can also be a combination of columns as well as a single column to identify a row.

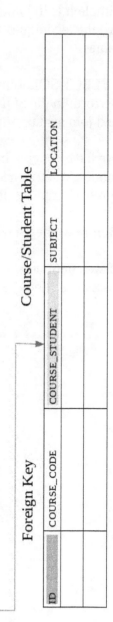

## Course/Student Table

Foreign Key

| ID | COURSE_CODE | COURSE_STUDENT | SUBJECT | LOCATION |
|---|---|---|---|---|
| | | | | |
| | | | | |

134

The course/student table has two important columns that need noting. The ID which will serve as the primary key for the table. However unlike the Student table the primary key is manually maintained and entered. This may be acceptable as the numbers of courses are relatively small and usually will have meaning to the organization. However the records entered into the course table can easily run into the thousands.

Fortunately Firebird supports automatic sequence numbering. That means that each time a record is inserted into that table it will be assigned the next number in the sequence of numbers automatically. That number will never be used again even if it has been deleted.

The other important column in the course/student table is the course_student column, which is the foreign key and serves the purpose of identifying what course(s) our student is taking. This means that a student can be on more than one course at anyone time. This type of relationship between the two tables is sometimes referred to as a 'one-to-many' relationship.

Also this table can record past courses students have been on, but that would require that we add additional fields to record start and end dates. We will expand on this in later chapters including the addition on the course table. We will also explain why and when we need to include information that could have been retrieved from other tables, e.g. why record course subject and location (performance issues and identify change). However for now we will start with our minimum data requirements.

Let us begin. Type and execute the following:

```
CREATE TABLE COURSE_STUDENT (
        id integer generated by default as identity
primary KEY,
        COURSE_CODE VARCHAR(100) NOT NULL,
        COURSE_STUDENT VARCHAR(100),
        SUBJECT VARCHAR(250),
```

```
      LOCATION VARCHAR(250)
   );
```

*Referential integrity…*

Now that we have created our course/student table, we want to
maintain some basic integrity, such as when we *delete* a student
then all the deletions cascade down the chain. Also if we
*update/change* key information then those updates/changes also
cascade down the chain. In the case of deletion it may not be the
case that you want to remove the dependent data. However
depending on your organisation and policy, purging/ archiving old,
dead records are a necessary and routine task that needs to be
performed. More on this in our maintenance chapter.

Perform the following task using DBeaver

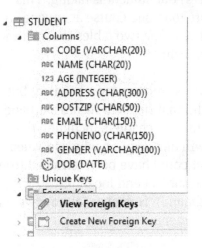

Select the student table, right-click
the Foreign Key, and select
Create New Foreign Key option

select the **COUSRE_STUDENT** table and populate the following
then click OK:

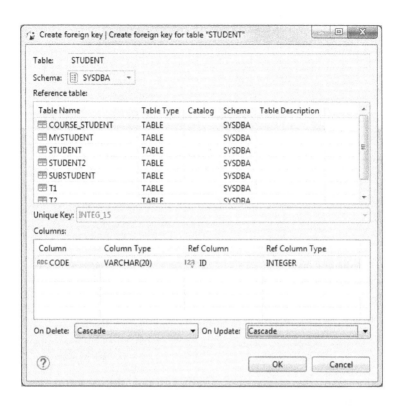

We can pictorially view the Entity-Relationship diagram (ER-Diagram) in DBeaver by performing the following:

Select the Course_Student tab and then select the ER-Diagram tab as shown below.

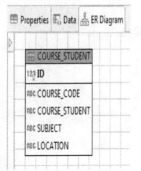

Now simply drag-drop the Student table to the grid page as shown

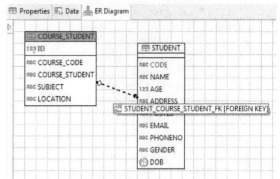

Here you can see the graphical representation of the relationship between the two tables.

Put another way, the referential integrity constraint is a constraint that is specific between two tables and is used to maintain the consistency among the records of the two tables.

Therefore, for referential integrity to hold in a relational database, any column in a base table that is declared a foreign key can contain either a NULL value, or only values from a parent table's primary key or a candidate key. In other words, when a foreign key value is used it must reference a valid, existing primary key in the parent table. For instance, deleting a record that contains a value referred to by a foreign key in another table would break referential integrity. Firebird, to a large extent, can enforce referential integrity, normally either by deleting the foreign key rows as well to maintain integrity, or by returning an error message and not performing the required 'delete' action.

Let us now return to Joining tables to demonstrate this point.

Now that we have created our course/student table we can begin adding useful information and continue to see SQL in action.
Add a Foreign Key to COURSE_STUDENT as follows:

```
ALTER TABLE COURSE_STUDENT ADD FOREIGN KEY
(COURSE_STUDENT) REFERENCES STUDENT(CODE) ON DELETE
CASCADE ON UPDATE CASCADE
```

Now check COURSE_STUDENT diagram you should be presented with the following:

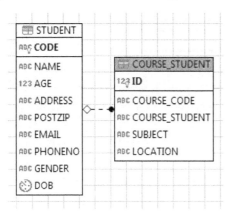

Let us begin by performing a check to see if our referential integrity is working correctly.

First we will add a somewhat older student. Type and execute the following;

```
INSERT INTO STUDENT
(CODE,NAME,AGE,ADDRESS,POSTZIP,EMAIL,PHONENO,GENDER,DOB)
        VALUES ('SE765','James Brown',11,'123456 Pitts
Avenue','I098

76X','j.brown@abcxyz.com','071434566','Male','1965-02-05');
```

Next type and execute the following:

```
INSERT INTO course_student
(course_code,course_student, subject, location)
VALUES ('XYZ01','SE765 ','Mathematics','Room Mtho2
Block');
```

We should have the following entry for COURSE_STUDENT:

| 123 ID | ABC COURSE_CODE | ABC COURSE_STUDENT | ABC SUBJECT | ABC LOCATION |
|--------|------------------|---------------------|-------------|--------------|
| 1 | 1 XYZ01 | SE765 | Mathematics | Room Mtho2 Block |

The STUDENT table will look similar to the screen presented below:

| | ABC CODE | ABC NAME | 123 AGE | ABC ADDRESS |
|---|----------|----------|---------|-------------|
| 1 | SK765 | John smith | 19 | 123456 Pitts Avenu |
| 2 | PH856 | Peter Hollis | 19 | 25 NEW York |
| 3 | DFRE3W | Mathew Syed | 18 | 12 Victoria Park, Cedar Sq, Milton Keynes |
| 4 | BHJHG | Fiona Jones | 20 | 54 Dyer Avenue |
| 5 | JH321 | Jane Headly | 21 | 14 Seymore Place |
| 6 | SE765 | James Brown | 11 | 123456 Pitts Avenue |

Therefore we can see that student 'James Brown' (SE765) is taking Mathematics, indicated by the foreign key entry in COURSE_STUDENT.
Now let us recap the constraint we placed on the foreign key:

```
DELETE CASCADE ON UPDATE CASCADE
```

We said that any changes we made in the parent (main) table we want to cascade to all tables it is referenced with.

First we will change the student code SE765 to SE765_1 by running the following SQL statement:

```
UPDATE student SET code='SE765_1' WHERE code='SE765';
```

Now, if all went well we should see the code change for COURSE_STUDENT in the COURSE_STUDENT table. We can perform a simple SELECT query to check this.

Type and execute the following:

```
SELECT * FROM course_student;
```

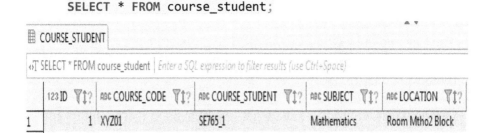

Here we can see that the change has reflected in the COURSE_STUDENT table. In other words, the Update constraint has worked ok.
Now what do you think would happen if you attempted to change the COURSE_STUDENT data in the COURSE_STUDENT table? In other words, what do you think would happen if you tried to run the following statement:

```
UPDATE course_student SET course_student='SE765_2'
WHERE code='SE765_1';
```

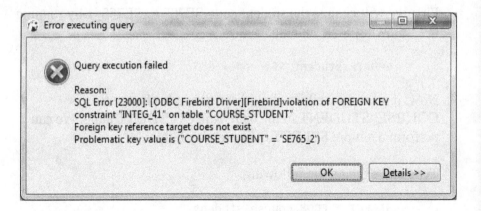

You guessed correctly, the statement will generate a foreign key violation, telling you that you cannot change this record because the referential integrity would be broken.

Our next test would be to see what would happen if we attempt to enter a course_student code that does not have an associated student entry in the student table.

Type and execute the following:

```
INSERT INTO course_student
(course_code,course_student, subject, location)
VALUES ('COMP98','CC765 ','Computer Science','Room
CS101 Block');
```

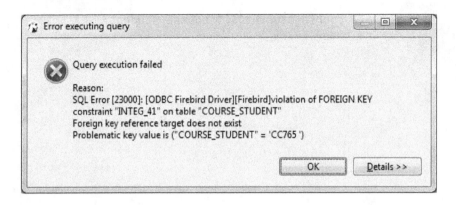

This generates a violation error that lets us know that Firebird could not find a reference 'CC765' in the student table.
This rejection ensures that only valid entries are entered into the COURSE_STUDENT table.

Our final test would be to make sure that when we delete that student from the student table then all cascade entries are removed. We test this by typing and executing the following:

```
DELETE FROM STUDENT WHERE code='SE765_1';
```

Now check the COURSE_STUDENT. `SELECT * FROM course_student;`

| 🗒 COURSE_STUDENT | | | | | |
|---|---|---|---|---|---|

T SELECT * FROM course_student | *Enter a SQL expression to filter results (use Ctrl+Space)*

| 123 ID ▽↕? | ᴬᴮᶜ COURSE_CODE ▽↕? | ᴬᴮᶜ COURSE_STUDENT ▽↕? | ᴬᴮᶜ SUBJECT ▽↕? | ᴬᴮᶜ LOCATION ▽↕? |
|---|---|---|---|---|
| | | | | |

You can now see the record has been deleted.

ⓘ The 'cascade delete' command may not always be the best option. Think very carefully before implementing this one. For example, what if you created a simple database for a medical practice that recorded patient details and their treatment. As human beings we tend to make mistakes from time to time. What would have happened if you implemented 'cascade delete' and by mistake you deleted the patient's main demographic details? Well, **all** their treatments will be deleted, **and** any other tables that have reference to it. (Hopefully you would have backed up prior to this important action). Usual practice would only allow an authorized user to make such critical deletions.

We are now satisfied that Firebird will maintain the integrity of the data. Let us now populate our COURSE_STUDENT table with courses that students are taking.
Type and execute the following *script*: (*remember*    )

```
INSERT INTO course_student (course_code,course_student, subject,
location) VALUES ('ENG101','SK765 ','Engineering','Room EE101
Block');

INSERT INTO course_student (course_code,course_student, subject,
location) VALUES ('COMP98','PH856 ','Computer Science','Room CS131
Block');

INSERT INTO course_student (course_code,course_student, subject,
location) VALUES ('AXA04','DFRE3W ','Architecture, landscape and
built environment','Axanar Dept');

INSERT INTO course_student (course_code,course_student, subject,
location) VALUES ('FEB76','BHJHG ','Law and
Criminology','Lancaster Lecture Threatre');

INSERT INTO course_student (course_code,course_student, subject,
location) VALUES ('HUM34','JH321 ','Humanities and Social
Science','Block HSL1');
```

```
SELECT * FROM course_student;
```

| | 123 ID | ABC COURSE_CODE | ABC COURSE_STUDENT | ABC SUBJECT | ABC LOCATION |
|---|---|---|---|---|---|
| 1 | 12 | AXA04 | DFRE3W | Architecture, landscape and built environment | Axanar Dept |
| 2 | 10 | ENG101 | SK765 | Engineering | Room EE101 Block |
| 3 | 11 | COMP98 | PH856 | Computer Sceince | Room CS131 Block |
| 4 | 13 | FEB76 | BHJHG | Law and Criminology | Lancaster Lecture Threatre |
| 5 | 14 | HUM34 | JH321 | Humanities and Social Science | Block HSL1 |

### Why we need to use Joins...

Due to the fact that our data is divided over multiple tables to aid in
a more efficient storage, better access and manipulation as well as
greater scaleability, we still need a way of relating data held in one
table with data held in another. In other words, we need a way of
joining our data together. We do this by using JOIN. Therefore we
can simply use joins within our SELECT statement to relate data
held in one table to data held in another.

### Creating Joins...

One of the simplest ways (although not the best) would be to simply
use the WHERE clause.

Let us see this in action:

Our first joined query would be to list the students by name and the course they are taking.

Type and execute the following:

```
SELECT code, name, subject, location
FROM student, course_student
WHERE student.code = course_student.course_student;
```

| | ABC CODE | ABC NAME | ABC SUBJECT | ABC LOCATION |
|---|---|---|---|---|
| 1 | SK765 | John smith | Engineering | Room EE101 Block |
| 2 | PH856 | Peter Hollis | Computer Science | Room CS131 Block |
| 3 | DFRE3W | Mathew Syed | Architecture, landscape and built environment | Axanar Dept |
| 4 | BHJHG | Fiona Jones | Law and Criminology | Lancaster Lecture Threatre |
| 5 | JH321 | Jane Headly | Humanities and Social Science | Block HSL1 |

The above example simply lists the columns taken from the tables in the FROM statement, unlike all our previous FROM statements here we have listed two tables, if we needed data from a third table then we must include the third table in the FROM statement.

In this example our WHERE clause simply looks for matches in the student.code with a match in the course_student.course_student columns.

Notice we used the fully qualified names for both tables in our WHERE statement. This is done if there is a likely chance of any ambiguity, that any chance of both tables having the same column name. Usual best practice is to always use fully qualified names both in the SELECT and WHERE if your query contains more than one table. This would aid in future-proofing if the table where to be altered in the future.

It is important to always join your tables. The above join will run down the first table and look for a match in the second table. This type of join is called an **equijoin** a join based on testing the equality between tables. What would we get if we forget to join the tables.

Consider the following:

```
SELECT code, name,subject,location
FROM student, course_student;
```

| | ᴀʙᴄ CODE ▽↕? | ᴀʙᴄ NAME ▽↕? | ᴀʙᴄ SUBJECT ▽↕? | ᴀʙᴄ LOCATION ▽↕? |
|---|---|---|---|---|
| 1 | SK765 | John smith | Architecture, landscape and built environment | Axanar Dept |
| 2 | SK765 | John smith | Engineering | Room EE101 Block |
| 3 | SK765 | John smith | Computer Sceince | Room CS131 Block |
| 4 | SK765 | John smith | Law and Criminology | Lancaster Lecture Threatre |
| 5 | SK765 | John smith | Humanities and Social Science | Block HSL1 |
| 6 | PH856 | Peter Hollis | Architecture, landscape and built environment | Axanar Dept |
| 7 | PH856 | Peter Hollis | Engineering | Room EE101 Block |
| 8 | PH856 | Peter Hollis | Computer Sceince | Room CS131 Block |
| 9 | PH856 | Peter Hollis | Law and Criminology | Lancaster Lecture Threatre |
| 10 | PH856 | Peter Hollis | Humanities and Social Science | Block HSL1 |
| 11 | DFRE3W | Mathew Syed | Architecture, landscape and built environment | Axanar Dept |
| 12 | DFRE3W | Mathew Syed | Engineering | Room EE101 Block |
| 13 | DFRE3W | Mathew Syed | Computer Sceince | Room CS131 Block |
| 14 | DFRE3W | Mathew Syed | Law and Criminology | Lancaster Lecture Threatre |
| 15 | DFRE3W | Mathew Syed | Humanities and Social Science | Block HSL1 |
| 16 | BHJHG | Fiona Jones | Architecture, landscape and built environment | Axanar Dept |
| 17 | BHJHG | Fiona Jones | Engineering | Room EE101 Block |
| 18 | BHJHG | Fiona Jones | Computer Sceince | Room CS131 Block |
| 19 | BHJHG | Fiona Jones | Law and Criminology | Lancaster Lecture Threatre |
| 20 | BHJHG | Fiona Jones | Humanities and Social Science | Block HSL1 |
| 21 | JH321 | Jane Headly | Architecture, landscape and built environment | Axanar Dept |
| 22 | JH321 | Jane Headly | Engineering | Room EE101 Block |
| 23 | JH321 | Jane Headly | Computer Sceince | Room CS131 Block |
| 24 | JH321 | Jane Headly | Law and Criminology | Lancaster Lecture Threatre |
| 25 | JH321 | Jane Headly | Humanities and Social Science | Block HSL1 |

We will get a result similar to the one shown above, where there is a n-set for each row of students.

If you can remember your high school set theory days, this is known as a *Cartesian product*, or in database-speak a 'cross join'. It would be very unlikely that you would want this. (And this is only with 5 rows of data). The message here is: remember to join your tables.

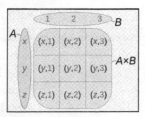

Cartesian product A × B of the sets
A = { x , y , z } and B = { 1 , 2 , 3 }

Courtesy of wiki

## INNER JOIN...

Another way of creating a simple equijoin, is to use an ***inner join*** as
follows:

```
SELECT code, name,subject,location
FROM student INNER JOIN course_student
ON student.code=course_student.course_student;
```

| | ᴬᴮᶜ CODE | ᴬᴮᶜ NAME | ᴬᴮᶜ SUBJECT | ᴬᴮᶜ LOCATION |
|---|---|---|---|---|
| 1 | SK765 | John smith | Engineering | Room EE101 Block |
| 2 | PH856 | Peter Hollis | Computer Science | Room CS131 Block |
| 3 | DFRE3W | Mathew Syed | Architecture, landscape and built environment | Axanar Dept |
| 4 | BHJHG | Fiona Jones | Law and Criminology | Lancaster Lecture Threatre |
| 5 | JH321 | Jane Headly | Humanities and Social Science | Block HSL1 |

This example produced exactly the same result as the previous
example. Here we simply inserted the INNER JOIN between the
tables and removed the comma on the FROM line, and replaced the
WHERE clause with the ON clause.

ⓘ In terms of performance there is no difference between them, in most cases.

In terms of readability, it is recommended to use the JOIN type. In
other words, this example clearly tells the reader what type of join
is being performed with this query. As your queries become more
complex this becomes more relevant.

148

There is no limit to the amount of tables that you can join in a SELECT statement. The rules are the same. We first list all the tables we want to use, then define the relationship between them.

To demonstrate this we need to create another table. This table will hold the details of the actual courses offered by the university. We will call this table *Course*.

Type and execute the following:

```
CREATE TABLE COURSE (
        id integer generated by default as identity
primary KEY,
        COURSE_CODE VARCHAR(100) NOT NULL,
        DESCRIPTION VARCHAR(250),
        SUBJECT VARCHAR(1500),
        CATTYPE VARCHAR(50),
        LOCATION VARCHAR(250),
        DURATION integer
);
```

Now type and execute the following:

```
CREATE INDEX COURSE_COURSE_CODE_IDX ON COURSE
(COURSE_CODE);
```

This creates an index key for the column course_code, which will also aid in performance.

We now need to populate our course table, therefore type and execute the following:

```
INSERT INTO course (course_code, description, subject,
cattype, location, duration)
VALUES ('AXA04','This course teach the student the..
','Architecture, landscape and built environment','BS
Hon','Axanar Dept',36);
```

```
INSERT INTO course (course_code, description, subject,
cattype, location, duration)
VALUES ('ENG101','General Students taking this course
will.. ','Engineering','Foundation','Room EE101 Block',12);

INSERT INTO course (course_code, description, subject,
cattype, location, duration)
VALUES ('COMP98','The latest in.. ','Computer Science','BS
Hon','Room CS131 Block',36);

INSERT INTO course (course_code, description, subject,
cattype, location, duration)
VALUES ('FEB76','Seen as a .. ','Law and Criminology','BA
Hon','Lancaster Lecture Threatre',36);

INSERT INTO course (course_code, description, subject,
cattype, location, duration)
        VALUES ('HUM34','Seen as a .. ','Humanities and
        Social Science','BA Hon','Block HSL1',36);
```

You should see the following screenshot

| ID | COURSE_CODE | DESCRIPTION | SUBJECT | CATTYPE | LOCATION | DURATION |
|----|-------------|-------------|---------|---------|----------|----------|
| 1 | 1 AXA04 | This course teach the student the.. | Architecture, landscape and built environment | BS Hon | Axanar Dept | 36 |
| 2 | 2 ENG101 | General Students taking this course will.. | Engineering | Foundation | Room EE101 Block | 12 |
| 3 | 3 COMP98 | The latest in.. | Computer Sceince | BS Hon | Room CS131 Block | 36 |
| 4 | 4 FEB76 | Seen as a .. | Law and Criminology | BA Hon | Lancaster Lecture Threatre | 36 |
| 5 | 5 HUM34 | Seen as a .. | Humanities and Social Science | BA Hon | Block HSL1 | 36 |

You can edit your own description (this is usually a summary of the course that appears in a university course prospectus).

Now let us return to our subject of joining multiple tables.

### *Joining multiple tables using WHERE...*

First we will look at using the WHERE clause. Consider the following:

```
SELECT code, description, name, cattype
FROM course, student, course_student
WHERE student.code=course_student.course_student AND
course.course_code=course_student.course_code;
```

‹›I SELECT code, description, name, cattype FROM co | Enter a SQL expression to filter results (use Ctrl-

| | ABC CODE ⍦⍰ | ABC DESCRIPTION ⍦⍰ | ABC NAME ⍦⍰ | ABC CATTYPE |
|---|---|---|---|---|
| 1 | SK765 | General Students taking this course will.. | John smith | Foundation |
| 2 | PH856 | The latest in.. | Peter Hollis | BS Hon |
| 3 | DFRE3W | This course teach the student the.. | Mathew Syed | BS Hon |
| 4 | BHJHG | Seen as a .. | Fiona Jones | BA Hon |
| 5 | JH321 | Seen as a .. | Jane Headly | BA Hon |

We can see that this is similar to our previous WHERE clause joining of two tables. Here we simply selected the list of columns we require and include another matching term in our *WHERE* clause along with the AND operator.

### *Joining multiple tables using INNER JOIN clause...*

```
SELECT code, description, name, cattype
FROM student INNER JOIN course_student INNER JOIN
course
ON course.course_code=course_student.course_code ON
course_student.course_student=student.code;
```

151

| | ABC CODE 〒↕? | ABC DESCRIPTION 〒↕? | ABC NAME 〒↕? | ABC CATTYPE |
|---|---|---|---|---|
| 1 | SK765 | General Students taking this course will.. | John smith | Foundation |
| 2 | PH856 | The latest in.. | Peter Hollis | BS Hon |
| 3 | DFRE3W | This course teach the student the.. | Mathew Syed | BS Hon |
| 4 | BHJHG | Seen as a .. | Fiona Jones | BA Hon |
| 5 | JH321 | Seen as a .. | Jane Headly | BA Hon |

Note the result is the same.

ⓘ A word of warning, the more tables you join the more resource intensive the search becomes, therefore only join tables that you need, or consider a trade off as we did by storing a copy of the location in our course_student table, where we know that location will be needed more very frequently.

From this example you will be correct if you thought that using joins will be, in most cases, more efficient than using sub-queries. However, there will be times that you will need sub-queries, and therefore it's best that you feel confident knowing how to use them.

We can also use the **WHERE** clause to filter the results. Consider the following:

```
SELECT code, description, name, cattype
FROM student INNER JOIN course_student INNER JOIN course
ON course.course_code=course_student.course_code ON
course_student.course_student=student.code
WHERE student.age >=21;
```

| | ABC CODE 〒↕? | ABC DESCRIPTION 〒↕? | ABC NAME 〒↕? | ABC CATTYPE |
|---|---|---|---|---|
| 1 | JH321 | Seen as a .. | Jane Headly | BA Hon |

We apply a filter listing students age 21 and above.
This example makes it clear what tables are joined and what table columns are filtered.

# 19  More on Joins

In the previous chapter we discussed basic ways we can join multiple tables. We mainly discussed the standard JOIN command, that is to say the INNER JOIN. In this chapter we will be looking at joining tables in more detail.

So let us recap on the joins you have learned so far. This we can depict graphically.

**INNER JOIN**

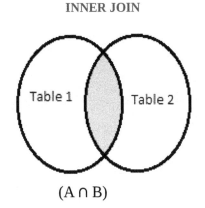

(A ∩ B)

The inner join where the selected column in each table row matches

**CROSS JOIN (Cartesian Product)**

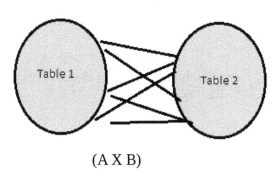

(A X B)

The Cross Join where every entry in table 1 cross links to every entry in table 2. Usually as a result of not remembering to include the *where* clause or *Join* operator.

Besides these two Joins, SQL allows us to use other joins to query our tables.

The following Joins are first best represented pictorially.

## Outer Joins...

Most joins are typically INNER JOINS where you would relate rows in one table with rows in another. However there are times where you may want to include rows that have no related rows. For example you may want to list all those students taking a course (but still including courses within that list that will show there are no students taking certain courses yet). SQL allows you to perform the following OUTER joins.

FULL OUTER JOIN

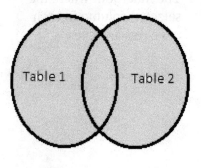

The full outer join when there is a match in table 1 _or_ table 2 (Left or Right).

ⓘ A word of warning. This type of join can return a very large result.

$$(A \cap B) \cup (A - B) \cup (B - A)$$

FULL OUTER JOIN

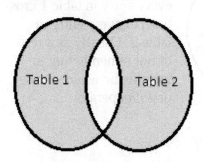

The full outer join when there is **no** match in table 1 _or_ table 2 (Left or Right).

ⓘ A word of warning. This type of join can also return a very large result.

## LEFT OUTER JOIN

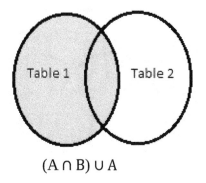

The LEFT JOIN returns all records from the left table (table1), and the matched records from the right table (table2). The result is NULL from the right side, if there is no match.

(A ∩ B) ∪ A

## RIGHT OUTER JOIN

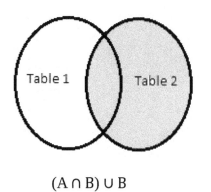

The RIGHT JOIN returns all records from the right table (table2), and the matched records from the left table (table1). The result is NULL from the left side, if there is no match.

(A ∩ B) ∪ B

### *Other Joins...*

Other than the inner and outer joins, there are a few more that are worth discussing.

## MINUS JOINS

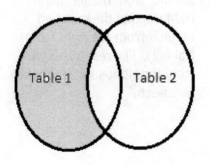 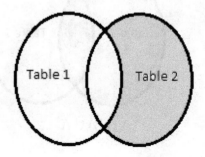

### SQL syntax

SELECT <select list...>
FROM tables
[WHERE conditions]
MINUS
SELECT <select list...>
FROM tables
[WHERE conditions];

## SELF JOIN

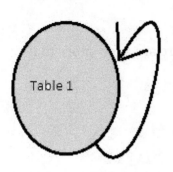

A self JOIN is a regular join, but the table is joined with itself.

For example, a student at the university may also be a member of staff. This is typical for Phd student, to give lectures to 1$^{st}$ year degree undergraduates.

## Natural Join...

You will be bound to come across the term 'NATURAL JOIN' as you continue to work with SQL databases.

### So what is a NATURAL JOIN?

We have already looked at how an INNER JOIN performs a JOIN, against equality or matching column(s) values of the associated tables and where an equal sign (=) is used as comparison operator in the WHERE clause, to refer to equality.

The SQL NATURAL JOIN is a type of INNER JOIN and is structured in such a way that, columns with the same name of associated tables will appear once only.

Whenever tables are joined, at least one column appears in more than one table (the columns being joined). Our INNER JOIN, for example, returns all data, even multiple occurrences of the same column. A NATURAL JOIN simply eliminates any additional occurrences, returning only one occurrence in each column. This is usually done with the wildcard (SELECT *) for one table and explicit subsets of the columns for all other tables.

For example type and execute the following:

```
SELECT course.*, course_student.course_student
FROM course INNER JOIN course_student
ON course.course_code=course_student.course_code;
```

| 123 ID | ABC COURSE_CODE | ABC DESCRIPTION | ABC SUBJECT | ABC CATTYPE | ABC LOCATION | 123 DURATION | ABC COURSE_STUDENT |
|---|---|---|---|---|---|---|---|
| 1 | AXA04 | This course teach the student the.. | Architecture, landscape and built environment | BS Hon | Axanar Dept | 36 | DFRE3W |
| 2 | ENG101 | General Students taking this course will.. | Engineering | Foundation | Room EE101 Block | 12 | SK765 |
| 3 | COMP98 | The latest in.. | Computer Science | BS Hon | Room CS131 Block | 36 | PH856 |
| 4 | FEB76 | Seen as a .. | Law and Criminology | BA Hon | Lancaster Lecture Threatre | 36 | BHJHG |
| 5 | HUMB4 | Seen as a .. | Humanities and Social Science | BA Hon | Block HSL1 | 36 | JH321 |

Notice that Course_Code column is only listed once.

Let us now consider how SQL allows us to perform some of the Outer Joins graphically presented above.
LEFT OUTER JOIN...

To demonstrate the LEFT JOIN we first need to insert another course in the course table.
Type and execute the following:

```
INSERT INTO course (course_code, description,
subject, cattype, location, duration)
VALUES ('ART256','Seen as a .. ','Fine Art And
Graphic Design','BA Hon','Block ABL2',36);
```

Now type and execute the following *Left Outer Join* SQL statement.

```
SELECT course.*, course_student.course_student
FROM course LEFT OUTER JOIN course_student
ON course.course_code=course_student.course_code;
```

| ) ID | ABC COURSE_CODE | ABC DESCRIPTION | ABC SUBJECT | ABC CATTYPE | ABC LOCATION | 123 DURATION | ABC COURSE_STUDENT |
|---|---|---|---|---|---|---|---|
| 1 | AXA04 | This course teach the student the.. | Architecture, landscape and built environment | BS Hon | Axanar Dept | 36 | DFRE3W |
| 2 | ENG101 | General Students taking this course will.. | Engineering | Foundation | Room EE101 Block | 12 | SK765 |
| 3 | COMP98 | The latest in.. | Computer Science | BS Hon | Room CS131 Block | 36 | PH856 |
| 4 | FEB76 | Seen as a.. | Law and Criminology | BA Hon | Lancaster Lecture Threatre | 36 | BHJHG |
| 5 | HUM34 | Seen as a.. | Humanities and Social Science | BA Hon | Block HSL1 | 36 | JH321 |
| 6 | ART256 | Seen as a.. | Fine Art And Graphic Design | BA Hon | Block ABL2 | 36 | [NULL] |

Notice that where there is no student taking a particular course the **COURSE_STUDENT** cell is *NULL*.

## *RIGHT OUTER JOIN...*

To demonstrate the RIGHT JOIN we first need to insert another course in the course table.
Type and execute the following:

```
INSERT INTO STUDENT
(CODE,NAME,AGE,ADDRESS,POSTZIP,EMAIL,PHONENO,GENDER,D
OB)
```

```
VALUES ('SE765','James Brown',11,'123456 Pitts
Avenue','I098

76X','j.brown@abcxyz.com','071434566','Male','1965-
02-05');
```

Now type and execute the following *Right Outer Join* SQL
statement.

```
SELECT code, name,subject,location,
course_student.course_code
FROM course_student RIGHT OUTER JOIN  student
ON student.code=course_student.course_student;
```

| | ᴀʙᴄ CODE | ᴀʙᴄ NAME | ᴀʙᴄ SUBJECT | ᴀʙᴄ LOCATION | ᴀʙᴄ COURSE_CODE |
|---|---|---|---|---|---|
| 1 | SK765 | John smith | Engineering | Room EE101 Block | ENG101 |
| 2 | PH856 | Peter Hollis | Computer Science | Room CS131 Block | COMP98 |
| 3 | DFRE3W | Mathew Syed | Architecture, landscape and built environment | Axanar Dept | AXA04 |
| 4 | BHJHG | Fiona Jones | Law and Criminology | Lancaster Lecture Threatre | FEB76 |
| 5 | JH321 | Jane Headly | Humanities and Social Science | Block HSL1 | HUM34 |
| 6 | SE765 | James Brown | [NULL] | [NULL] | [NULL] |

Again notice that the student information is listed but this student is
also not taking any course.

## Self Join...

Another join that is worth mentioning is the SELF JOIN. As
mentioned before you may need to use the SELF JOIN in situations
where an entity can play two roles, for example where a student can
also play the role of a lecturer or an employee can also be a
supervisor within a company.

But before we discuss details of SELF JOIN, we need to take a
short detour to look at table 'aliases'.

*What are Table Aliases?...*

In previous chapters we used column 'aliases' to represent our calculated fields or to rename column names in our resultant SQL statement.

Recap, for example, we simply do the following:

```
SELECT code, name AS StudentName FROM student;
```

| ABC CODE | ABC STUDENTNAME |
|----------|-----------------|
| SK765 | John smith |
| PH856 | Peter Hollis |
| DFRE3W | Mathew Syed |
| BHJHG | Fiona Jones |
| JH321 | Jane Headly |
| SE765 | James Brown |

Where column *name* has an alias *StudentName*.

ⓘ Note, in Firebird the **AS** operator is optional, however it is best practice to include the *AS* for its portability.

Aliases are not just limited to table columns. We can also use aliases for whole tables. The main reasons why we would want to use aliases for tables are:

I.   To shorten the query syntax, and
II.  To allow multiple uses of the same table within a single SELECT statement.
III. To use within sub-queries.

Consider the following examples, the first is without an alias.

```
SELECT course.*, course_student.course_student
FROM course LEFT OUTER JOIN course_student
ON course.course_code=course_student.course_code;
```

Rewritten using aliases, this example illustrates how we may use aliases to shorten the SQL syntax statement.

```
SELECT c.*, cs.course_student
FROM course AS c LEFT OUTER JOIN course_student AS cs
ON c.course_code=cs.course_code;
```

As already mentioned, another reason why we may use table aliases is to allow multiple uses of the same table within a single SELECT statement. This is the case for *self join* queries.

To illustrate the SELF JOIN, let us suppose that one of the course locations needs urgent repairs and that this will take several months to complete. Therefore we want to locate all students who would be taking lectures at that location. We therefore could simply create the following SQL query statement:

```
SELECT cs1.course_code, cs1.course_student
FROM course_student AS cs1, course_student AS cs2
WHERE cs1.course_student=cs2.course_student
AND cs2.location='Block HSL1';
```

| ABC COURSE_CODE ▼↕? | ABC COURSE_STUDENT |
| --- | --- |
| HUM34 | JH321 |

*Aggregate Functions and Joins...*

In previous chapters we saw how to use aggregate functions within our single query statements. We can still perform aggregate functions in the same way on joined tables.

Consider the following example:

```
SELECT code, name,dob, ROUND(TRUNC(age,0)) age, course_code
FROM course_student INNER JOIN
(
        SELECT code,name, dob, IIF(leapyear=0, datediff(day,
dob,CURRENT_DATE) /                    365.22,datediff(day,
dob,CURRENT_DATE) / 365.20)  AS age
```

```
      FROM
      (
      SELECT  code, name, dob,MOD(EXTRACT (YEAR FROM
CURRENT_DATE),4) AS leapyear
      FROM student
      ) AS sub

) AS subsub ON subsub.code = course_student.course_student;
```

| ABC CODE ▼↕? | ABC NAME ▼↕? | ⊙ DOB ▼↕? | 123 AGE ▼↕? | ABC COURSE_CODE |
|---|---|---|---|---|
| DFRE3W | Mathew Syed | 2000-06-25 | 17 | AXA04 |
| SK765 | John smith | 1999-03-02 | 19 | ENG101 |
| PH856 | Peter Hollis | 1999-01-25 | 19 | COMP98 |
| BHJHG | Fiona Jones | 1998-09-28 | 19 | FEB76 |
| JH321 | Jane Headly | 1997-11-14 | 20 | HUM34 |

This example may appear a little complex at first but it is simply an
extension on an example you came across in chapter 17, working
with sub-queries.

Also note that Joins can also be used with the **WHERE** clause to
further filter the results.

# Summing up chapters 14 to 19

We have covered a lot in the last six chapters. This would be a good place to summarize these chapters.

## Chapter 14 - Data Manipulation Functions.

Here we looked at how Firebird SQL supports data manipulation. The types of functions that Firebird supports are Text manipulation, Mathematical functions, Date/time functions, Boolean Logic and system manipulation functions. These functions can all be included in your SQL statements. We rounded up the chapter with a brief discussion on Firebird's external functions also referred to as User-Defined Functions (UDF).

## Chapter 15 - Summarizing Data

This chapter focused more on Firebird's Aggregate Functions.

Along with Data Manipulation Functions, it is often necessary to summarize some or all of our data without retrieving it all. Firebird provides functions for that purpose. By using these functions we can retrieve data for analysis purposes. For example, we can produce reports to:

• Retrieve the number of rows in a table.
• Obtain the sum of a group of rows in a table
• Find the Maximum, Minimum or Average value in a table column.

Firebird's aggregate functions are AVG, COUNT, LIST, MAX, MIN, and SUM.

We looked at various examples to illustrate each one.

### *Chapter 16 - Grouping Data*

Often it is necessary to group Data into various categories. One example we looked at was grouping by gender and another by age groups.

We saw how using the GROUP BY clause we then introduced the HAVING filter, as the WHERE clause can only be used before the GROUPING.
We looked at examples demonstrating the ordering of WHERE, GROUP BY, and HAVING.

### *Chapter 17 - Working with Sub-queries.*

We now moved on from our simple queries and looked at the topic of sub-queries also known as 'inner' or 'nested' queries.

Sub-queries allow us the ability to perform operations in multiple steps. For example, if you wanted to take the sums of several columns, then average all of those values, you'd need to do each aggregation in a distinct step.

Sub-queries can, for example, be used to aggregate in multiple stages.

We briefly touched on how we can join sub-queries, using the JOIN operator.

We also looked at how we can combine conditional criteria within our sub-query using the IIF and CASE operators.

### *Chapters 18 – Joins*

We delved deeper into 'joins' and how to use them. We looked at the various joins from INNER, OUTER, LEFT, RIGHT, MINUS, etc. By the end of chapter 18 the reader should be very familiar with how to construct queries out of two of more tables.

We looked at the importance of Foreign Keys and their role along with how to setup referential integrity constraints.

***Chapter 19***. We continued our discussion on Joins by giving a little context to their use and the various types of Joins that Firebird supports.

# 20  Compound Queries

Firebird and most other SQL DBMSs, contain a single SELECT statement that returns data from one or more tables. Combining multiple SELECT query results is performed by using the UNION operators.

To use this UNION clause, each SELECT statement must have:-

- The same number of columns selected
- The same number of column expressions
- The same data type and
- Have them in the same order

But they need not have to be in the same length.

In a compound query, you can combine the queries by adding their results together, subtracting the results of one query from the other, or intersecting the results to find only the accounts or entries that exist in both queries.

### *Creating Compound Queries...*

In SQL we create compound queries using the *UNION* operator, in which multiple *SELECT* statements can be specified, and their results can be combined giving a single result.

### *The UNION operator...*

Let us consider the following example using the *UNION* operator:

```
SELECT course.COURSE_CODE, course.subject, course.LOCATION,
course_student.course_student
FROM course LEFT OUTER JOIN course_student
ON course.course_code=course_student.course_code

UNION
```

```
SELECT course_student.COURSE_CODE, subject,location,
course_student.course_student
FROM course_student RIGHT OUTER JOIN  student
ON student.code=course_student.course_student;
```

| | ABC COURSE_CODE | ABC SUBJECT | ABC LOCATION | ABC COURSE_STUDENT |
|---|---|---|---|---|
| 1 | [NULL] | [NULL] | [NULL] | [NULL] |
| 2 | ART256 | Fine Art And Graphic Design | Block ABL2 | [NULL] |
| 3 | AXA04 | Architecture, landscape and built environment | Axanar Dept | DFRE3W |
| 4 | COMP98 | Computer Science | Room CS131 Block | PH856 |
| 5 | ENG101 | Engineering | Room EE101 Block | SK765 |
| 6 | FEB76 | Law and Criminology | Lancaster Lecture Threatre | BHJHG |
| 7 | HUM34 | Humanities and Social Science | Block HSL1 | JH321 |

As you can see, writing a compound query simply means writing
multiple **SELECT** queries and combining them using the **UNION**
as long as the rules are obeyed.

We can further explain the **UNION** operator, by looking at two
queries separately and then combining the results.

Consider Query1:

```
SELECT code, name, age FROM student WHERE age < 17;
```

| | ABC CODE | ABC NAME | 123 AGE |
|---|---|---|---|
| 1 | SE765 | James Brown | 11 |

Query 2:

```
SELECT code, name, age FROM student WHERE age IN (19,
21)
```

| | ᴬᴮᶜ CODE ⍦↕? | ᴬᴮᶜ NAME ⍦↕? | 123 AGE ⍦↕? |
|---|---|---|---|
| 1 | SK765 | John smith | 19 |
| 2 | PH856 | Peter Hollis | 19 |
| 3 | JH321 | Jane Headly | 21 |

Now using the **UNION** operator as follows:

```
SELECT code, name, age FROM student WHERE age < 17
UNION
SELECT code, name, age FROM student WHERE age IN (19,
21);
```

Note we remove (;) (statement terminator) from the first select statement.

| | ᴬᴮᶜ CODE ⍦↕? | ᴬᴮᶜ NAME ⍦↕? | 123 AGE ⍦↕? |
|---|---|---|---|
| 1 | JH321 | Jane Headly | 21 |
| 2 | PH856 | Peter Hollis | 19 |
| 3 | SE765 | James Brown | 11 |
| 4 | SK765 | John smith | 19 |

Here the UNION simply combines both query results into one single SELECT resultant query result.

The first **SELECT** query (query 1) finds student who are aged under 17 "gifted students". The second query **SELECT** (query 2) uses the **IN** to find students age 19 or 21.

We then used the **UNION** to combine both queries.

You may have noticed that we could have got the same result had we simply used multiple WHERE criteria. In other words we could simply do the following:

```
SELECT code, name, age FROM student WHERE age < 17 OR
age IN (19, 21);
```

This would give the same resultant result as shown above.

Consider the following:

```
SELECT age FROM student WHERE age < 17
UNION
SELECT age FROM student WHERE age IN (19, 21);
```

| | 123 AGE ▼↕? |
|---|---|
| 1 | 11 |
| 2 | 19 |
| 3 | 21 |

This query is the same UNION query presented previously, minus the code and name columns. Notice that this UNION only returns three resultant records. This is because the **UNION** also eliminates duplicate records. If we want to see all the records then we must use the **ALL** clause with the **UNION** operator, as shown here:

```
SELECT age FROM student WHERE age < 17
UNION ALL
SELECT age FROM student WHERE age IN (19, 21);
```

| | 123 AGE ▼↕? |
|---|---|
| 1 | 11 |
| 2 | 19 |
| 3 | 19 |
| 4 | 21 |

The **ALL** will then list all records. Therefore the WHERE equivalent is the **UNION ALL**.

### ORDER BY ...

The sorting must come at the end of the last SELECT query, therefore if for example the first query had an ORDER BY clause then it will need to be removed or placed at the end. For example, if we wanted to sort (in other words, order) our rows by age we will need to do this as follows:

```
SELECT code, name, age FROM student WHERE age < 17
UNION
SELECT code, name, age FROM student WHERE age IN (19,
21) ORDER BY 3 DESC;
```

| | ᴀʙᴄ CODE ▽↕? | ᴀʙᴄ NAME ▽↕? | 123 AGE ▽↕? |
|---|---|---|---|
| 1 | JH321 | Jane Headly | 21 |
| 2 | PH856 | Peter Hollis | 19 |
| 3 | SK765 | John smith | 19 |
| 4 | SE765 | James Brown | 11 |

An important point to note here, is to notice that, when using the UNION of multiple SELECT commands in Firebird, we cannot reference the column by name but by the index position in the SELECT list.

Consider the following, if using the 'column name' for example:

```
SELECT code, name, age FROM student WHERE age < 17
UNION
SELECT code, name, age FROM student WHERE age IN (19,
21) ORDER BY age DESC;
```

executing the following will produce the following exception error:

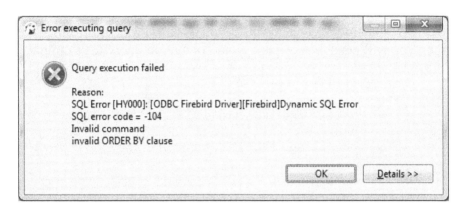

However, if you really want to order the results using the 'column name' then you can nest the query in a SELECT query i.e. sub-query, for example:

```
SELECT code, name, age
FROM
(
  SELECT code, name, age FROM student WHERE age < 17
  UNION
  SELECT code, name, age FROM student WHERE age IN (19,21)
)
ORDER BY age DESC;
```

| | ABC CODE | ABC NAME | 123 AGE |
|---|---|---|---|
| 1 | JH321 | Jane Headly | 21 |
| 2 | PH856 | Peter Hollis | 19 |
| 3 | SK765 | John smith | 19 |
| 4 | SE765 | James Brown | 11 |

### *Limiting the results...*

You may recall that if we want to limit the number of resulting rows
from our SELECT query then we use Firebird's FIRST clause.
Unlike other RDMBSs such as MariaDB, MySQL, MS SQL Server,
etc. limiting the resultant list in Firebird means you simply add the
LIMIT x keyword to the end of the SELECT command..

However, Firebird requires that you use FIRST just after the
SELECT statement. This means if you wish to limit your result
then you will need to sub-query your compound query for example:

```
SELECT FIRST 2 age
FROM (
        SELECT age FROM student WHERE age < 17
        UNION ALL
        SELECT age FROM student WHERE age IN (19, 21)
);
```

| | 123 AGE ▼↕? |
|---|---|
| 1 | 11 |
| 2 | 19 |

This ends our chapter on compound queries using the SQL *UNION*
operator.

# 21  Using Full-Text Searching

Over the years one question that keeps popping up is, 'Does Firebird support Full-Text Search?'

Well, not directly in the engine, but there are third-party solutions:

Three that are very good are:

- Sphinx - http://www.sphinxsearch.com/downloads/current/
- Mutis - https://sourceforge.net/projects/mutis/
- dotLucene - https://sourceforge.net/projects/dotlucene/

### *What is Full-Text Searching...?*

In chapter 9 we used SQL wildcards '*' and '%' to filter our data. In chapter 9 the *LIKE* keyword was introduced. We used the *LIKE* operator to match text (or partial text). Using *LIKE*, we were able to locate rows that contained specific text or parts of text, regardless of where they are located within the row columns.

In chapter 10 we expanded text searching and introduced "regular expressions" text-based searching. As we saw using regular expressions it was possible to write sophisticated matching patterns to locate our data.

However, as great as these mechanisms may be, they do have a few limitations:

- Performance – Due to the fact that each and every row in the table needs to be matched it can result in time-consuming searches. Therefore both wildcard and regular expression matching suffer from performance issues, particularly in very large tables.

- Explicit controls – Consider for example, within a single operation you want to search for a specific word, and a word that must not be matched and also a word you may or may not need to be matched if the first word resulted in a match. Using wildcard or regular expressions could be very confusing and therefore difficult.

- Intelligent results – Wildcards and regular expressions are not necessarily intelligent search mechanisms:

  they are unable to return such things as related words to your search if it was unable to find your specific match. Furthermore, searches using wildcard or regular expressions usually result in all or nothing, it will not distinguish if a row has a single or multiple match.

What we need is a mechanism that will address all these and more limitations. Full-Text searching does exactly that.

In this chapter we will be looking at a third-party Full-Text search engine called Sphinx which fully supports Firebird.

Why use Sphinx...

Sphinx is a very powerful and popular free open source full-text search engine.

Some of the benefits for choosing Sphinx are:

- It is truly open source.
- Easy to setup.
- Low memory foot print.
- Talks directly to a Firebird database.
- Support ODBC connection.
- Supported on most platforms (Windows, Linux, and Mac).
- Based on delta indexing.
- Large online support community.

- Mature over 18 years development and used by large organizations.

*Installing Sphinx...*

Download and install Sphinx from:
http://sphinxsearch.com/downloads/current/  - Current version specific to your hardware.

Older versions you can obtain from:
http://sphinxsearch.com/downloads/archive/

Create a folder and unzip the file in that folder. The file structure should be similar as shown below:

For linux users you will need to compile your version. Information on how to do this is found here:
http://sphinxsearch.com/docs/current.html#compiling-source-linux

### *Setting up the environment...*

Before we can use Sphinx we need to setup the environment. To do this perform the following steps:

Sphinx comes with an example SQL script. We need to import this into our database.

In DBeaver select *File → Import → General → File System → Next*

Populate the following screen as necessary to where you unzipped Sphinx then click Finish

You will now see that the example script has been added as shown below:

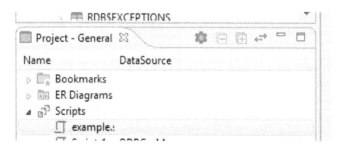

Double-clicking on the example will display the script we need to execute:

```
DROP TABLE IF EXISTS test.documents;
CREATE TABLE test.documents
(
        id                      INTEGER PRIMARY KEY NOT NULL
AUTO_INCREMENT,
        group_idINTEGER NOT NULL,
        group_id2       INTEGER NOT NULL,
        date_added      DATETIME NOT NULL,
        title           VARCHAR(255) NOT NULL,
        content         TEXT NOT NULL
);

REPLACE INTO test.documents ( id, group_id, group_id2, date_added,
title, content ) VALUES
        ( 1, 1, 5, NOW(), 'test one', 'this is my test document
number one. also checking search within phrases.' ),
        ( 2, 1, 6, NOW(), 'test two', 'this is my test document
number two' ),
        ( 3, 2, 7, NOW(), 'another doc', 'this is another
group' ),
        ( 4, 2, 8, NOW(), 'doc number four', 'this is to test
groups' );

DROP TABLE IF EXISTS test.tags;
CREATE TABLE test.tags
(
        docid INTEGER NOT NULL,
        tagid INTEGER NOT NULL,
        UNIQUE(docid,tagid)
);

INSERT INTO test.tags VALUES
        (1,1), (1,3), (1,5), (1,7),
        (2,6), (2,4), (2,2),
        (3,15),
```

177

```
(4,7), (4,40);
```

Before executing the script we need to modify it.

First remove the word *test. (the Dot needs to be removed also)*

Comment out also the DROP statement as Firebird does not support IF EXISTS yet.

Summary:

- --DROP TABLE IF EXISTS documents;
- CREATE TABLE documents
- id INTEGER generated by default as identity primary key,
- date_added TIMESTAMP NOT NULL,
- content CHAR(2000) NOT NULL
- REPLACE INTO documents (....    change to UPDATE OR INSERT INTO documents (
- DROP TABLE tags;
- --DROP TABLE IF EXISTS tags;
- CREATE TABLE tags
- INSERT INTO tags VALUES
- NOW() change to CURRENT_TIMESTAMP

Note, unlike MSSQL Server, MYSQL, MariaDB, etc, Firebird still does not support INSERT INTO for multiple values therefore you will need to modify both INSERT INTO statements to separate lines.

Therefore the final script as shown below.

```
--DROP TABLE IF EXISTS documents;
CREATE TABLE documents
(
--      id                      INTEGER PRIMARY KEY NOT NULL
AUTO_INCREMENT,
        id integer generated by default as identity primary KEY,
        group_idINTEGER NOT NULL,
        group_id2       INTEGER NOT NULL,
        date_added      TIMESTAMP NOT NULL,
        title           VARCHAR(255) NOT NULL,
        content         CHAR(2000) NOT NULL
);

UPDATE OR INSERT INTO documents (id, group_id, group_id2,
date_added, title, content) VALUES
        ( 1, 1, 5, CURRENT_TIMESTAMP, 'test one', 'this is my test
document number one. also checking search within phrases.');
```

```
UPDATE OR INSERT INTO documents (id, group_id, group_id2,
date_added, title, content) VALUES
        ( 2, 1, 6, CURRENT_TIMESTAMP, 'test two', 'this is my test
document number two');
UPDATE OR INSERT INTO documents (id, group_id, group_id2,
date_added, title, content) VALUES
        ( 3, 2, 7, CURRENT_TIMESTAMP, 'another doc', 'this is
another group');
UPDATE OR INSERT INTO documents (id, group_id, group_id2,
date_added, title, content) VALUES
        ( 4, 2, 8, CURRENT_TIMESTAMP, 'doc number four', 'this is
to test groups');

--DROP TABLE tags;
CREATE TABLE tags
(
        docid INTEGER NOT NULL,
        tagid INTEGER NOT NULL,
        UNIQUE(docid,tagid)
);

INSERT INTO tags (docid,tagid) VALUES (1,1);
INSERT INTO tags (docid,tagid) VALUES (1,3);
INSERT INTO tags (docid,tagid) VALUES (1,5);
INSERT INTO tags (docid,tagid) VALUES (1,7);
INSERT INTO tags (docid,tagid) VALUES (2,6);
INSERT INTO tags (docid,tagid) VALUES (2,4);
INSERT INTO tags (docid,tagid) VALUES (2,2);
INSERT INTO tags (docid,tagid) VALUES (3,15);
INSERT INTO tags (docid,tagid) VALUES (4,7);
INSERT INTO tags (docid,tagid) VALUES (4,40);
```

Click the 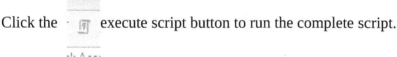 execute script button to run the complete script.

Now that we have created and populated our documents and tags tables we can now continue setting up sphinx.

1. Navigate to your *etc.* folder and copy *sphinx-min.conf.dist* to the bin folder.

2. Rename *sphinx-min.conf.dist* in the *bin* folder to *sphinx.conf* Note the full .conf file is quite large and can be confusing for beginners. You can use it for reference. For the purpose of this book the minimum version is good enough.

179

3. Our next step is to configure our minimum sphinx.conf file. You can connect to sphinx in a number of ways. Fortunately for us, we can continue to use our odbc dsn connection.

The main line to note in the .conf file is as follows:

```
odbc_dsn =
DSN=MyFirebird;Driver={C:/Windows/ODBCINST.INI};Uid=SYSDBA;Pw
d=masterkey
```

Notice the driver points to the c:/windows/odbcinst.ini file. Also note the (/) in Windows Sphinx does not seems to mind if you use (/ or \)

Rather than go through line-by-line of how to configure the .conf file, the file will be shown below:

```
#
# Minimal Sphinx configuration sample (clean, simple, functional)
#

source src1
{
    type        = odbc

    sql_host = localhost
    sql_user = sysdba
    sql_pass = masterkey
    sql_db = c:/myapp/data/myapp.fdb


        odbc_dsn =
DSN=MyFirebird;Driver={C:/Windows/ODBCINST.INI};Uid=SYSDBA;Pwd=masterkey

        sql_query                = SELECT id, group_id, date_added, title,
content FROM documents

        sql_attr_uint           = group_id
        sql_attr_timestamp      = date_added
        sql_column_buffers      = content=12M, comments=1M
}

index test1
{
        source                  = src1
        path                    = c:/sphinx/sphinx-3.0.3/text1
}

indexer
{
        mem_limit               = 128M
}
searchd
{
        listen                  = 9312
        listen                  = 9306
```

```
log                              = c:/sphinx/sphinx-3.0.3/searchd.log
query_log                    = c:/sphinx/sphinx-3.0.3/query.log
read_timeout      = 5
max_children      = 30
pid_file          = c:/sphinx/sphinx-3.0.3/bin/sphinxdata/searchd.pid
seamless_rotate   = 1
preopen_indexes   = 1
unlink_old           = 1
workers              = threads # for RT to work
binlog_path          = c:/sphinx/sphinx-3.0.3
}
```

Now depending on where you have installed Sphinx you will need to modify accordingly.

One important point to note here is that columns that are non text need to be defined. Thus note group_id and date_added to instruct Sphinx that these are non text columns.

Now, if everything is setup correctly we begin using Sphinx, but before we do, let us take a look at our current folder. Navigate to your sphinx folder as shown below:

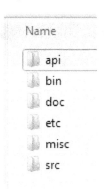

You should see main default six folders. The main programs and tools are located in the bin folder. Navigate to the bin folder and you will see the following executable files.

Now navigate back up to the root folder of Sphinx with the six folders as shown above.

Now open your terminal / console and navigate to the Sphinx bin folder. Try and get in background view the sphinx root folder as shown below:

| Name | Date modified | Type | Size |
|------|---------------|------|------|
| api | 04/05/2018 15:43 | File folder | |
| bin | 09/07/2018 10:48 | File folder | |
| doc | 04/05/2018 15:43 | File folder | |
| etc | 04/05/2018 15:43 | File folder | |
| misc | 04/05/2018 15:43 | File folder | |
| src | 04/05/2018 15:43 | File folder | |

```
Administrator: C:\Windows\system32\cmd.exe

C:\sphinx\sphinx-3.0.3\bin>indexer --rotate --all_
```

Now the first things we need to do is run the indexer file. Therefore type and execute the following:

```
Administrator: C:\Windows\system32\cmd.exe

C:\sphinx\sphinx-3.0.3\bin>indexer --rotate --all
```

If your .conf file was configured correctly you should get the following:

```
C:\sphinx\sphinx-3.0.3\bin>indexer --rotate --all
Sphinx 3.0.3-dev (commit facc3fb)
Copyright (c) 2001-2018, Andrew Aksyonoff
Copyright (c) 2008-2016, Sphinx Technologies Inc (http://sphinxsearch.com)

using config file './sphinx.conf'...
indexing index 'test1'...
collected 4 docs, 0.0 MB
sorted 0.0 Mhits, 100.0% done
total 4 docs, 8.0 Kb
total 0.1 sec, 87.2 Kb/sec, 43 docs/sec
WARNING: failed to open pid_file 'c:/sphinx/sphinx-3.0.3/bin/sphinxdata/searchd.
pid'.
WARNING: indices NOT rotated.

C:\sphinx\sphinx-3.0.3\bin>_
```

We can ignore the warning message for now, as the 'searchd'
daemon program is not running.

You should also notice in the background additional files added to
the sphinx folder as shown
below:

| | |
|---|---|
| api | 04/05/2018 15:43 |
| bin | 09/07/2018 10:48 |
| doc | 04/05/2018 15:43 |
| etc | 04/05/2018 15:43 |
| misc | 04/05/2018 15:43 |
| src | 04/05/2018 15:43 |
| text1.new.sha | 09/07/2018 11:03 |
| text1.new.spa | 09/07/2018 11:03 |
| text1.new.spd | |
| text1.new.spe | |
| text1.new.sph | |
| text1.new.spi | |
| text1.new.spj | |
| text1.new.spk | |
| text1.new.spp | |

```
Administrator: C:\Windows\system

C:\sphinx\sphinx-3.0.3\bin
Sphinx 3.0.3-dev (commit f
Copyright (c) 2001-2018, A
Copyright (c) 2008-2016, S

using config file './sphin
indexing index 'test1'...
collected 4 docs, 0.0 MB
sorted 0.0 Mhits, 100.0% d
total 4 docs, 8.0 Kb
total 0.1 sec, 78.8 Kb/sec
WARNING: failed to open pi
pid'.
WARNING: indices NOT rotat

C:\sphinx\sphinx-3.0.3\bin
```

If you did not get this to work, the most likely cause will be our
**sphinx.conf** file settings.

Our next step is to install the 'searchd' daemon program.

To install the 'searchd' daemon type and execute the following:

```
C:\sphinx\sphinx-3.0.3\bin>searchd --install --config c:\sphinx\sphinx-3.0.3\bin
\sphinx.conf --servicename mysphinx
```

```
C:\sphinx\sphinx-3.0.3\bin>searcd --install --config c:\sphinx\sphinx-3.0.3\bin\
sphinx.conf --servicename mysphinx
'searcd' is not recognized as an internal or external command,
operable program or batch file.

C:\sphinx\sphinx-3.0.3\bin>searchd --install --config c:\sphinx\sphinx-3.0.3\bin
\sphinx.conf --servicename mysphinx
Sphinx 3.0.3-dev (commit facc3fb)
Copyright (c) 2001-2018, Andrew Aksyonoff
Copyright (c) 2008-2016, Sphinx Technologies Inc (http://sphinxsearch.com)

Installing service...
Service 'mysphinx' installed successfully.
```

Let us check if we have installed the 'searchd' as a service
(Windows users only) go to Windows services and check for the
'searchd' entry as follows:

| mysphinx | mysphinx-3.0.3-dev (commit fa... | Automatic | Local Syste... |

Notice the 'searchd' program service has not been started yet. We
will leave it that way for now.

We will start the 'searchd' daemon manually. This will give us a
better insight as to what is going on.

Type and execute the following:

```
C:\sphinx\sphinx-3.0.3\bin>searchd --config sphinx.conf
```

This starts our 'searchd' daemon with our sphinx.conf file in the bin
(same) folder.

You should get the following response:

```
C:\sphinx\sphinx-3.0.3\bin>searchd --config sphinx.conf
Sphinx 3.0.3-dev (commit facc3fb)
Copyright (c) 2001-2018, Andrew Aksyonoff
Copyright (c) 2008-2016, Sphinx Technologies Inc (http://sphinxsearch.com)

using config file 'sphinx.conf'...
listening on all interfaces, port=9312
listening on all interfaces, port=9306
precaching index 'test1'
rotating index 'test1': success
precached 1 indexes in 0.023 sec
WARNING: No extra index definitions found in data folder
prereading 1 indexes
prereaded 1 indexes in 0.000 sec
accepting connections
```

Sphinx is now running and listening for a connection on port 9312 and 9306. If you experience any problems here then it is likely that your firewall is blocking these ports. If so then simply create a rule in your firewall settings to accept these ports.

Note: Linux users can also simply execute the same 'searchd' daemon as a service, remembering to use full name and path and also remembering that Linux is case-sensitive.

You should also notice, in the background, three additional files have been created:

> binlog.meta
>
> query.log
>
> searchd.log

Now type **ctrl+c** to stop the 'searchd' daemon, and start the 'searchd' service (Windows user).

Linux uses the two most common commands which are:

```
sudo systemctl start searchd –config sphinx.conf
```

or

```
sudo service searchd -config sphinx.conf start
```

If neither command works then check your user manual (or google search "How to start, stop, and restart services in Linux").

If you get the following error:

Create folders **data** and **log** in your sphinx root folder

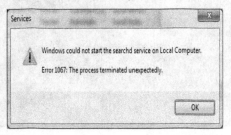

If all is well then go ahead and *right mouse-click* on mysphinx service and *select* start

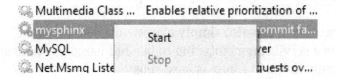

This service should start as shown below:

### Sphinx working with Firebird...

In this section we will be looking at how to get Sphinx to query our document table in our database.

As we are learning about Sphinx we will stop mysphinx service and call it from command-line.
This will allow us to monitor what is happening in the background.

We will be using php runtime for our test.
If you do not have php already loaded on your computer then download it from:

https://windows.php.net/download select the latest zip file.

Create a folder for example C:\php7 and extract the files in the folder, e.g.

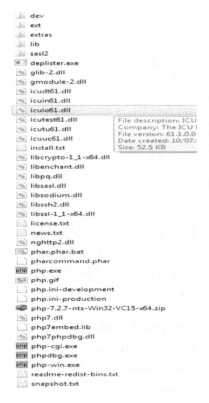

The main file we will be running is php.exe.

For Linux users php usually is installed by default therefore if it is not already running simply start the service.

Now lets take a look at the api folder within Sphinix. Navigate to your Sphinx api folder e.g.

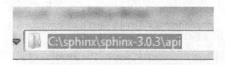

You should see the following folders and files:

Sphinx comes with a few example back-end codes. However they can be a little confusing if your'e not familiar with this scripting languages. Therefore we will roll our own very simple php script which I am sure you will be able to follow.

First open your preferred text editor, for example vi for Linux users or notepad for Windows users and type the following php text and save it in the api folder with the name *search.php*.

```php
<?php
        require ( "sphinxapi.php" );

        $sphinxClient = new sphinxClient();
```

```
      $sphinxClient -> setServer('localhost',9312);
?>
```

Basically, the first line of all php scripts must start with '<?php' and end (last line) with '?>'.

Take a look at the files in the api folder and you will see one called sphinxapi.php. Our script will be using classes (information) from that file, namely sphinxClient, hence the line *"requires sphinx.php"*

The next two lines simply create an instance of sphinxClient and point the client to our Sphinx server engine, which we will start manually later.
The next step is to start a php server (session). To do this, perform the following steps:

From within your terminal console navigate to the Sphinx api folder type and execute the following:

c:\php7\php.exe -S localhost:8000

```
C:\sphinx\sphinx-3.0.3\api>c:\php7\php.exe -S localhost:8000
PHP 7.2.7 Development Server started at Fri Jul 13 12:43:55 2018
Listening on http://localhost:8000
Document root is C:\sphinx\sphinx-3.0.3\api
Press Ctrl-C to quit.
```

This will open a session that you can browse on port 8000.

Open our web browser and type the url as follows:

189

If you get a blank screen then everything is working ok.

Now we can manually start the Sphinx server. Open another terminal window and navigate to the Sphinx bin folder and simply type searchd or (searchd.exe windows users only).

Now we will modify our *search.php* script, adding the following two lines

```
$results = $sphinxClient->query('test');
print_r($results);
```

Your complete php script should be as follows:

```
<?php

        require ( "sphinxapi.php" );

        $sphinxClient = new sphinxClient();
        $sphinxClient -> setServer('localhost',9312);

        $results = $sphinxClient->query('test');
        print_r($results);

?>
```

Here we are searching for the word 'test' in our document table.

Now refresh your browser and you should get the following reply:

```
Array ( [error] => [warning] => [status] => 0 [fields] => Array
( [0] => title [1] => content ) [attrs] => Array ( [group_id] => 1
[date_added] => 2 ) [matches] => Array ( [1] => Array ( [weight] =>
2421 [attrs] => Array ( [group_id] => 1 [date_added] => 2018 ) ) [2]
=> Array ( [weight] => 2421 [attrs] => Array ( [group_id] => 1
[date_added] => 2018 ) ) [4] => Array ( [weight] => 1442 [attrs] =>
Array ( [group_id] => 2 [date_added] => 2018 ) ) ) [total] => 3
[total_found] => 3 [time] => 0.000 [words] => Array ( [test] =>
Array ( [docs] => 3 [hits] => 5 ) ) )
```

To make this a little more readable simply right-mouse click on the page and select:

## *View Selection Source* as shown below

```
<html><head></head><body>Array
        (
            [error] =&gt;
            [warning] =&gt;
            [status] =&gt; 0
            [fields] =&gt; Array
                (
                    [0] =&gt; title
                    [1] =&gt; content
                )

            [attrs] =&gt; Array
                (
                    [group_id] =&gt; 1
                    [date_added] =&gt; 2
                )

            [matches] =&gt; Array
                (
                    [1] =&gt; Array
                        (
                            [weight] =&gt; 2421
                            [attrs] =&gt; Array
                                (
                                    [group_id] =&gt; 1
                                    [date_added] =&gt; 2018
                                )

                        )

                    [2] =&gt; Array
                        (
                            [weight] =&gt; 2421
                            [attrs] =&gt; Array
                                (
                                    [group_id] =&gt; 1
                                    [date_added] =&gt; 2018
                                )

                        )

                    [4] =&gt; Array
                        (
                            [weight] =&gt; 1442
                            [attrs] =&gt; Array
```

```
                    (
                        [group_id] =&gt; 2
                        [date_added] =&gt; 2018
                    )

                )

            )

        [total] =&gt; 3
        [total_found] =&gt; 3
        [time] =&gt; 0.000
        [words] =&gt; Array
            (
                [test] =&gt; Array
                    (
                        [docs] =&gt; 3
                        [hits] =&gt; 5
                    )

            )

    )
    </body></html>
```

As you can see it has returned some results, scroll to the bottom and you will see totals. It shows that in the docs table there are three rows that have test and there are five hits.

Under the matches section you will see [1] =&gt; Array where [1] will represent the index row there for this it telling us the index row [1], [2], and [4] found matches, and the totals are shown at the end.

We can confirm this by opening DBeaver and simply view the documents table as follows:

| 123 ID | 123 GROUP_ID | 123 GROUP_ID2 | DATE_ADDED | ABC TITLE | ABC CONTENT |
|---|---|---|---|---|---|
| 1 | 1 | 5 | 2018-06-29 11:27:35 | test one | this is my test document number one. also checking search within phrases. |
| 2 | 1 | 6 | 2018-06-29 11:27:35 | test two | this is my test document number two |
| 3 | 2 | 7 | 2018-06-29 11:27:35 | another doc | this is another group |
| 4 | 2 | 8 | 2018-06-29 11:27:35 | doc number four | this is to test groups |

As we can see rows 1 and 2 have two hits both in title and content and row 4 in content only giving a total of five matches (hits).

Now take a look at the query.log file, you should have similar entry as follows:

```
...8 2018] 0.000 sec 0.000 sec [ext/0/rel 3 (0,20)] [*] test
```

This shows that 3 records were found which matched our search word test.

Now change the search word in our *search.php* script to say test2, save it and refresh the webpage. Now re-examine the view source page and then check the query.log file by closing and re-openning it.

This time you will notice a second entry similar to the entry shown below:

```
… 2018] 0.000 sec 0.000 sec [ext/0/rel 0 (0,20)] [*] test2
```

Notice this time no results where found.

You should be able to see by now how powerful Sphinx can be, unlike the other text search we used previously, Sphinx can search the complete table across millions of rows and columns you wish to include in the indexing.

As an example, the following website https://www.offers.com/ uses Sphinx entirely for its full text searching.

Play around with the *search.php* script query word. Populate the documents table in the database.

Also play around with the sphinx.conf file (see the full conf file for what you can include).

Note that each time you change the conf file you must re-index using the indexer.

We will end this chapter here. It was a lot to take in, but I hope an interesting chapter.

As you can imagine we have barely scratched the surface of how useful Sphinx can be in our application. If you are interested in Sphinx then I recommed you visit: http://sphinxsearch.com/ where you will find a wealth of information, latest releases, a resource centre, a very healthy online community and much more.

# 22 Firebird Views

*What is Views...*

Put simply, Views are virtual tables. Views can be considered as simple containers used to contain queries that can be used to dynamically retrieve data when required.

To understand Views let's look at an example. In chapter 19 we looked at the following query:

```
SELECT code, name,dob, ROUND(TRUNC(age,0)) age, course_code
FROM course_student
INNER JOIN
(
  SELECT code,name, dob, IIF(leapyear=0, datediff(day,
dob,CURRENT_DATE) / 365.22,datediff(day, dob,CURRENT_DATE) /
365.20)  AS age
FROM
    (
      SELECT  code, name, dob,MOD(EXTRACT (YEAR FROM
       CURRENT_DATE),4)  AS leapyear
      FROM student
       ) sub

) AS subsub ON subsub.code = course_student.course_student;
```

which includes joins and sub-queries. Now, anyone wishing to use this query would have to understand the structure of the query and the tables. It would be great if we could put the query in a container, assign it a name and then when someone wished to use it, they would simply call it by it's name.

Firebird implements the SQL views. Views do not contain any actual tables, but instead they simply contain SQL queries.

Therefore, if we were to create a view of the above query, giving it the name *studentcoursewithage,*
then we could simply construct the following SQL statement using Views

SELECT * from *studentcoursewithage* ORDER BY age;

This example shows how to use Views. Other reasons for using Views are:

- To reveal only parts of a table, instead of the complete table.

- Encapsulation - restricting direct access to the underlining tables, adding a level of data security.

- To reformat and change the representation of the data.

- To reuse SQL statements. (re-usability).

- To simplify complex SQL queries as shown in the above example.

- Views provide an abstraction layer to the underlying data.

Once you have created a View you can use it in the same way, as you would with SQL SELECT statements.

However Views do have some restrictions on how they can be used.

### Criteria for using Views...

Unlike actual tables, Views do have certain rules and restrictions governing their usage and creation. Below is a list of the more common ones.

- Views must be uniquely named. (i.e. they cannot have the same names as another View or table in the database).

- Like queries, Views can be Sub-Views (nested).

- ORDER BY can be used in Views, but it can be overridden if ORDER BY is contained in the underlining query.

- Views cannot be indexed, nor have triggers, or have default values.

- Tables and Views can be used in combination within an SQL statement using JOINS.

*Creating Views in Firebird...*

In Firebird and most SQL RDBMSs, Views are created using the SQL CREATE VIEW command.

Type and execute the following:

```
CREATE VIEW studentcoursewithage AS
     SELECT code, name,dob, ROUND(TRUNC(age,0)) age,
course_code
     FROM course_student INNER JOIN
     (
        SELECT code,name, dob, IIF(leapyear=0,
     datediff(day, dob,CURRENT_DATE) /365.22,datediff(day,
     dob,CURRENT_DATE) / 365.20) AS age
      FROM
     (
       SELECT code, name, dob,MOD(EXTRACT (YEAR FROM
     CURRENT_DATE),4) AS leapyear
       FROM student
     ) sub

     ) AS subsub ON subsub.code =
course_student.course_student;
```

Now type and execute the following:

```
SELECT * FROM studentcoursewithage;
```

| | ABC CODE ▼↕? | ABC NAME ▼↕? | ⊙ DOB ▼↕? | 123 AGE ▼↕? | ABC COURSE_CODE |
|---|---|---|---|---|---|
| 1 | DFRE3W | Mathew Syed | 2000-06-25 | 17 | AXA04 |
| 2 | SK765 | John smith | 1999-03-02 | 19 | ENG101 |
| 3 | PH856 | Peter Hollis | 1999-01-25 | 19 | COMP98 |
| 4 | BHJHG | Fiona Jones | 1998-09-28 | 19 | FEB76 |
| 5 | JH321 | Jane Headly | 1997-11-14 | 20 | HUM34 |

Now type and execute the following:

```
SELECT * FROM studentcoursewithage ORDER BY age DESC;
```

| | ABC CODE ▼↕? | ABC NAME ▼↕? | ⊙ DOB ▼↕? | 123 AGE ▼↕? | ABC COURSE_CODE |
|---|---|---|---|---|---|
| 1 | JH321 | Jane Headly | 1997-11-14 | 20 | HUM34 |
| 2 | BHJHG | Fiona Jones | 1998-09-28 | 19 | FEB76 |
| 3 | PH856 | Peter Hollis | 1999-01-25 | 19 | COMP98 |
| 4 | SK765 | John smith | 1999-03-02 | 19 | ENG101 |
| 5 | DFRE3W | Mathew Syed | 2000-06-25 | 17 | AXA04 |

In this example we simply used Views to simplify a complex query and to have it presented as ORDER BY age formatted in descending order.

### *Using Views with substring manipulation...*

Type and execute the following:

```
SELECT code,dob, name,age,
        CAST(substring(code||'#' similar '%#"[[:DIGIT:]]+#"%'
        escape '#') AS INT) AS getNumber
from studentcoursewithage WHERE CAST(substring(code||'#'
similar '%#"[[:DIGIT:]]+#"%' escape '#') AS INT) IS NOT
null;
```

198

| ABC CODE | DOB | ABC NAME | 123 AGE | 123 GETNUMBER |
|---|---|---|---|---|
| SK765 | 1999-03-02 | John smith | 19 | 765 |
| PH856 | 1999-01-25 | Peter Hollis | 19 | 856 |
| DFRE3W | 2000-06-25 | Mathew Syed | 17 | 3 |
| JH321 | 1997-11-14 | Jane Headly | 20 | 321 |

In this example we use Views with string functions to retrieve the number part of the code column data.

It is quite common to use Views with aggregate, function and other tables in a single SQL statement.

### Using views with tables...

As mentioned above Views can be used with tables. Consider the following example:

```
SELECT sage.name, cs.location
FROM studentcoursewithage AS sage INNER JOIN
COURSE_STUDENT AS cs
ON sage.code = cs.course_student;
```

| ABC NAME | ABC LOCATION |
|---|---|
| Mathew Syed | Axanar Dept |
| John smith | Room EE101 Block LOCATI( |
| Peter Hollis | Room CS131 Block |
| Fiona Jones | Lancaster Lecture Threatre |
| Jane Headly | Block HSL1 |

This example simply joins our *studentcoursewithage* with the COURSE_STUDENT table. We further used aliases view and table names in this example.

## Using views with the WHERE clause...

Like tables, the SQL WHERE clause can be used with views. For example consider the following:

```
SELECT code, dob, name, age
FROM studentcoursewithage
WHERE age = 17;
```

| ᴀʙᴄ CODE ⵟⵜ? | ⏲ DOB ⵟⵜ? | ᴀʙᴄ NAME ⵟⵜ? | 123 AGE ⵟⵜ? |
|---|---|---|---|
| DFRE3W | 2000-06-25 | Mathew Syed | 17 |

The above example illustrates how we can filter the data using the WHERE clause.

## Using Views with calculated fields...

Again, like tables, views can be used with calculated fields.

You may recall that our view contains an age column which is a calculated field, we can further use that field to perform part of a calculation, treating it as just another field, for example consider the following:

```
SELECT code, dob, name, (age * 2) AS double_age
FROM studentcoursewithage;
```

| ᴀʙᴄ CODE ⵟⵜ? | ⏲ DOB ⵟⵜ? | ᴀʙᴄ NAME ⵟⵜ? | 123 DOUBLE_AGE ⵟⵜ? |
|---|---|---|---|
| DFRE3W | 2000-06-25 | Mathew Syed | 34 |
| SK765 | 1999-03-02 | John smith | 38 |
| PH856 | 1999-01-25 | Peter Hollis | 38 |
| BHJHG | 1998-09-28 | Fiona Jones | 38 |
| JH321 | 1997-11-14 | Jane Headly | 40 |

Purely as an example we simply performed a calculation on age.

*Updating Views...*

You may be wondering by now that, if Views are like tables, can Views update data?

Technically yes, but this does depend on the underlying query. If Views are a simple 'window' to a table, then Views can use INSERT, UPDATE, and DELETE operations. Because Views themselves do not contain any data, but simply have queries that use the table, then performing an update on a View, will simply update the underlying table.

For example the View `studentcoursewithage` cannot be updated, it is a read-only query. As a rule Views cannot be updated if they contain any of the following.

- GROUP BY and HAVING
- JOINS
- Sub-queries
- UNIONS
- Aggregate functions
- DISTINCT
- Calculated fields

For good practice, Views should not be used for updating unless you know for sure what table will be affected. After all, Views are primarily used for retrieving data.

**More on View manipulation**

*Deleting Views...*

Like tables Views can be deleted from the database by issuing a DROP <view> command.

*RECREATE VIEW...*

If a View with the same name already exists, RECREATE VIEW will try to drop it and create a new View. RECREATE VIEW will fail if the existing View is in use.

### ALTER VIEW...

ALTER VIEW, allowing you to change a View's definition without having to drop it first. Existing dependencies are preserved.

`d` `i` `y` *Things to try...*

1/ Create a View for the STUDENT table, name it *view_student.*
2/ perform an insert on *view_student* View.
3/ use RECREATE VIEW to replace it with the same name in (1)
4/ use ALTER VIEW and change the *view_student.*
5/ delete the View using the DROP command.

# 23  Working with Stored Procedures / Scalar Functions

So far, all the examples we have discussed have been simple single SQL statements.

Now, what if you needed to execute multiple statements, and these statements needed to be executed in order and could also be dependent on certain conditions being met?

For this situation, Firebird and most, but not all DBMSs, provide a mechanism call 'stored procedures' to handle this.

### *What are Stored Procedures and Stored Scalar Functions?...*

Stored procedures are coded modules of statements that can be executed in a couple of ways. Most major DBMSs support stored procedures.

In Firebird, stored procedures can be called by the client, by another stored procedure or by a trigger. Firebird stored procedures and triggers are written in Procedural SQL (PSQL).

It should be noted that Firebird's stored procedures can accept and return multiple parameters.

So, in what scenarios would we use stored procedures?

Consider the following:

- To process a request to withdraw a book from the university library, checks needs to be performed to ensure the book is on the shelves.

- If the book is available you need to reserve it so it is not given to someone else and the available stock quantity level needs to be adjusted accordingly.

- If the book is not available then either it is still out with another student or it needs to be ordered in if it is not stocked. Some intervention is needed here.

- The student needs to be notified on when he/she can expect the book to be in the library.

As you can see performing these task requires many Firebird statements to be executed. Now instead of having to write these as individual statements and having to execute them every time a book withdrawal is requested, we could somehow bundle them up in a batch file (technically it is more than a batch file), and execute the bundle.

This is where stored procedures come into play. In a nut shell stored procedures allow you to group your Firebird statements into a collection for future use.

### *What are the Benefits of using Stored Procedures...*

- The can be used to centralise user access logic into a single places. Making it easy for DBA's to optimize.

- Security benefits in that you can grant execute rights to a stored procedure but the user will not need to have read/write permissions on the underlying tables. This is a good first step against SQL injection.

- It simplifies complex tasks by wrapping the multiple tasks into a single reusable module.

- Stored procedures reduce network traffic and increase the performance.

- If we modify a stored procedure all the clients will get the updated stored procedure.

- Stored procedures execute faster than individual SQL statements, reduce network traffic and therefore stored procedures improve performance.

- A stored procedure allows modular programming. You can create the procedure once, store it in the database, and call it any number of times in your program.

Simply put, Firebird stored procedures offer: security, improved performance and simplicity in a single module.

However, stored procedures do have their downside.

- Maintenance associated with your basic CRUD *(stands for Create, Retrieve, Update, and Delete)* operation can be quite involved.

- Stored procedures tend to be quite complex to write. You need to be fairly skilled at writing stored procedures.

### *Using Firebird Stored Procedures...*

By doing a few examples, we can see how to create and execute various stored procedures.

Firebird  Stored Procedure (SP) Syntax

```
CREATE PROCEDURE procname
    [(<inparam> [, <inparam> ...])]
    [RETURNS (<outparam> [, <outparam> ...])]
AS
    [<declarations>]
BEGIN
    [<PSQL statements>]
END
```

Firebird also has introduced the concept of a Stored Function since version 3.0.  It is now possible to write a scalar function in PSQL and call it just like an internal function.

Syntax

```
        {CREATE [OR ALTER] | ALTER | RECREATE}
FUNCTION <name>
        [(param1 [, ...])]
        RETURNS <type>
        AS
        BEGIN
          ...
        END
```

Let us now create some procedures in Firebird.

Note that although DBeaver allows you to view stored procedures, unfortunately in the current version 5.0.0 there is not the facility for creating stored procedures. Therefore we will use isql for creating our stored procedures.

ⓘ Note because we are using Firebird in embedded mode you will have to exit DBeaver first before connecting to myapp.fdb via isql and visa versa when reconnecting with DBeaver.

Perform the following:

Exit DBeaver and run isql from the command prompt (konsole for linux users)

Run isql

and type the following:

```
connect c:\myapp\data\myapp.fdb user
SYSDBA password masterkey; then hit return
```

Note that this time the connection string and user/password are in one complete string:

206

```
SQL> connect c:\myapp\data\myapp.fdb user SYSDBA password masterkey;
Database: c:\myapp\data\myapp.fdb, User: SYSDBA
```

Now we will create a simple stored procedure to add two numbers together that we pass to the procedure.

Now before we begin, there is one key thing to understand.

**SET TERM**

In Firebird, because every command in an SQL script must be terminated by a semi-colon, the stored procedure itself, must too. To distinguish the semi-colons in the procedure from the terminating semi-colon, we need to assign a different terminator for the end of the procedure. This is done with SET TERM:

SET TERM !! ;
CREATE PROCEDURE x AS BEGIN ... END !!
SET TERM ; !!

Basically SET TERM !! ; instructs Firebird to use !! as the terminator and not; and SET TERM ; !! simply reverses it i.e. to change it back.
At the isql prompt is the following:

```
SQL> SET TERM !! ;
SQL> CREATE PROCEDURE MyAdd (a INTEGER, b INTEGER)
CON> RETURNS (Result INTEGER)
CON> AS BEGIN
CON> Result = a + b;
CON> END !!
SQL> SET TERM ; !!
SQL>
```

We can now test our procedure by typing the following:

EXECUTE PROCEDURE MyAdd (3,5);

```
SQL> EXECUTE PROCEDURE MyAdd(3,5);

       RESULT
=============
          8
```

207

By executing our stored procedure it returns the results.

As noted earlier, in Firebird 3.0 you can also create stored scalar Functions in PSQL. We will discuss this later on in this chapter.

To delete a stored procedure you simply issue a DROP PROCEDURE <name>; SQL statement. We will leave our MyAdd for now.

Exit iqsl and launch Dbeaver.

Expand the procedures folder and you should see our MyAdd procedure.

Type and execute the following:

`EXECUTE PROCEDURE MyAdd(2,5);`

| 123 RESULT ▽Ⅰ? |
|---|
| 7 |

Now exit DBeaver and launch isql and connect to the myapp.fdb database. Now delete our MyAdd procedure by typing and executing the following:

```
DROP PROCEDURE MyAdd;
```

*Working with parameters and SQL...*

We have seen from the previous example how to pass parameters to our stored procedure and get a return. This example demonstrates how by using INTO clause can pass results from our SQL statements to our parameters which will return the results from the stored procedure.

Type and execute the following:

```
SQL> SET TERM !! ;
SQL> CREATE PROCEDURE MYSTUD
CON> RETURNS (PMIN INTEGER, PMAX INTEGER, PAUG INTEGER)
CON> AS BEGIN
CON> SELECT MIN(AGE) FROM STUDENT INTO PMIN;
CON> SELECT MAX(AGE) FROM STUDENT INTO PMAX;
CON> SELECT AUG(AGE) FROM STUDENT INTO PAUG;
CON> END !!
SQL> SET TERM ; !!
SQL>
```

Now execute the stored procedure by typing and executing the following:

EXECUTE PROCEDURE MYSTUD;

Results should appear as shown below;

```
SQL> execute procedure mystud;

         PMIN          PMAX          PAUG
   ============  ============  ============
           11            21            18
```

In this example we bundled three simple SELECT statements into one procedure.

*Using repeat Loops...*

The ability to execute a section of your code several times is an important function in many programs. The action may be repeated

209

*for* a given number of times, or *until* a condition no longer holds true or may be repeated *while* a condition holds true.

PSQL allows you the ability to perform repeated steps multiple times.

Firebird has support for repeating steps with the *FOR* and *WHILE* statements.

To give a simple demonstration for each we will create a test table with only two fields.

Type and execute the following:

```
create table looptest (
  id int,
  Name char(150)
);
```

You can check to see if the table has been created by typing *show tables;* at isql prompt.

Now let us populate the table using first the *for* loop then followed by the *while* loop statements within our stored procedures.

### Using the for loop...

Now Type and execute the following as shown below:

```
SQL> set term !! ;
SQL> create procedure forloop
CON> as
CON> declare variable tmpname varchar(150);
CON> declare variable x int;
CON> begin
CON> x = 1;
CON> for select name from student into tmpname
CON> do
CON> begin
CON> insert into looptest (id,name) values(:x, :tmpname);
CON> x = x + 1;
CON> end
CON> end !!
SQL> set term ; !!
```

210

This should now create our *forloop* test procedure. To check if it has been created simply type **show procedures**, this will list all the procedures in our database.

Now type and execute the following:

```
SQL> execute procedure forloop;
SQL>
```

This will run the *forloop* procedure.

To check the results, type and execute the following:

*Select * from looptest;*

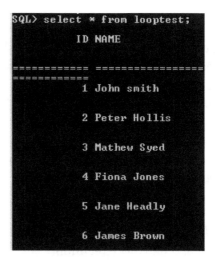

```
SQL> select * from looptest;
        ID NAME

============= =================
=============
         1 John smith

         2 Peter Hollis

         3 Mathew Syed

         4 Fiona Jones

         5 Jane Headly

         6 James Brown
```

Analysis

```
set term !! ;
    create procedure forloop
    as
    declare variable tmpname varchar(150);
    declare variable x int;
     begin
      x = 1;
      for select name from student into tmpname
      do
      begin
```

211

```
       insert into looptest (id,name) values (:x,
   :tmpname);
       x = x + 1;
     end
   end !!
set term ; !!
```

The above *forloop* procedure has been re-written for clarity.
We first needed to declare two variables *tmpname* (to hold the
student name) and *x* (as a counter).

Note that Variable declarations are declared after AS, and before the
first BEGIN.

Before we enter our for loop we give *x* an initial start value of 1. We
began our *forloop* for each row in the student table. That is to say
we execute "statement(s)" for every line that is returned by the
SELECT statement. Everything within the 'begin' and 'end' of the
*forloop* is repeated.

Each time we repeat the *forloop* we increment the *x* variable by 1
and insert it, along with the student name that we retrieved from the
student table, into the looptest table.

Since the *forloop* has reached the end to the student table, it ends
the *forloop* execution. The program comes to the final end in this
program and ends its execution.

### Using the whileloop...

This next example will be a slight modification to our *forloop*
example to demonstrate the *whileloop*.

But first delete all the records in the looptest table, type and execute
as follows;

*delete from looptest;*

Now type and execute the following:

```
SQL> set term !! ;
SQL> create procedure whileloop
CON> as
CON> declare variable tmpname varchar(150);
CON> declare variable x int;
CON> declare variable reccount int;
CON> declare cur cursor for (select name from student);
CON> begin
CON> open cur;
CON> x=1;
CON> select count(*) from student into :reccount;
CON> while (x <= reccount) do
CON> begin
CON> fetch cur into :tmpname;
CON> insert into looptest (id, name) values (:x, :tmpname);
CON> x=x+1;
CON> end
CON> close cur;
CON> end !!
SQL> set term ; !!
```

This would now create our *whileloop* procedure.

Now type and execute:

SET TERM ; !!

Now execute the *whileloop* procedure.

```
SQL> execute procedure whileloop;
```

```
SQL> select * from looptest;
    ID NAME

============ =================
============
     1 John smith

     2 Peter Hollis

     3 Mathew Syed

     4 Fiona Jones

     5 Jane Headly

     6 James Brown
```

213

```
set term !! ;
    create procedure whileloop
    as
    declare variable tmpname varchar(150);
    declare variable x int;
    declare variable reccount int;
    declare cur cursor for (select name from student);
    begin
     open cur;
     x=1;
     select count(*) from student into :reccount;
     while (x <= reccount) do
     begin
      fetch cur into :tmpname;
      insert into looptest (id, name) values (:x,
   :tmpname);
      x=x+1;
     end
     close cur;
    end !!
set term ; !!
```

This example as you can see is a little more involved. There is one variable we introduce here which is the 'cursor'. We will be looking at cursors in the next chapter devoted to cursors.

We declared as before our *tmpname* and *x* variables, however we also declared two additional variables:
reccount for holding the number of records in the student table and cur the cursor for now we will refer to it as an index into the positioning of the records for to select query, and each time we fetch a record the cursor (index) moves to the next record after it has returned the data requested.

Noticed that we needed to open the cursor (query) for reading, therefore when the program is finished it needs to be closed.

The rest of the program is very similar to the *forloop* example presented earlier.

### Inspecting our stored procedures...

To take a look at our stored procedure simply type and execute the following:

*show procedure whileloop;*

as shown below.

```
SQL> show procedure whileloop;
```

You should be presented with a similar screen as shown below.

```
Procedure text:
========================================================================
declare variable tmpname varchar(150);
declare variable x int;
declare variable reccount int;
declare cur cursor for (select name from student);
begin
open cur;
x=1;
select count(*) from student into :reccount;
while (x <= reccount) do
begin
fetch cur into :tmpname;
insert into looptest (id, name) values (:x, :tmpname);
x=x+1;
end
close cur;
end
========================================================================
SQL>
```

*Stored Functions...*

### What is a Firebird Stored function...?

It is a scalar function written in PSQL. It can be called similarly to an internal function. So why do we need to use them? Stored functions and stored procedures are technically the same. However there are a few reasons why you should consider using a stored function over a stored procedure.

215

- They are easier to call than stored procedures.
- They are more flexible than stored procedures with simpler nesting.

### *Easier to call...*

Consider the following stored procedure:

```
SELECT
 (SELECT output_column FROM  PSQL_PROC(T.col1)) AS col3,
 col2
FROM T
```

Now consider the stored function equivalent:

```
SELECT
 PSQL_FUNC(T.col1, T.col2) AS col3,
 col3
FROM T
```

As you may have observed, calling a stored function is as simple as calling an UDF function.

Creating  a stored function is slightly different from that of stored procedure.

Syntax as follows:

```
{CREATE [OR ALTER] | ALTER | RECREATE} FUNCTION <name>
    [(param1 [, ...])]
    RETURNS <type>
    AS
    BEGIN
     ...
    END
```

For example:

216

```
CREATE or ALTER FUNCTION StudAge(X INT) RETURNS
  INT
AS
BEGIN
  RETURN X+1;
END;
SELECT StudAge(17) FROM Student;
```

### More flexible...

When nesting multiple stored procedures, steps can quickly become very confusing particularly when nested using the **WHERE** clause. Stored functions makes it easier for nesting.

We will end our discussion on stored Functions / Procedures.

### stored procedure Commands summary...

| Command | Description |
|---------|-------------|
| **BEGIN** `<statements>` **END** | Compound Statement |
| `variable = expression` | Assignment. "variable" can be a local variable, an "in" or an "out" parameter. |
| `compound_statement` | A single command or a BEGIN/END block |
| `select_statement` | Normal SELECT statement. The INTO clause must be present at the end of the statement. Variable names can be used with a colon preceding them. Example:<br><br>`SELECT PRICE FROM ARTICLES`<br>`WHERE ARTNO = :ArticleNo`<br>`INTO :EPrice` |
| `/* Comment */` | Comment |

| | |
|---|---|
| `-- Comment` | Single line SQL comment |
| **DECLARE VARIABLE** `name datatype [= startval]` | Variable declaration. After AS, before the first BEGIN. |
| **EXCEPTION** | Re-fire the current exception. Only makes sense in WHEN clause |
| **EXCEPTION** `name [message]` | Fire the specified exception. Can be handled with WHEN. |
| **EXECUTE PROCEDURE** `name arg, arg` **RETURNING_VALUES** `arg, arg` | Calling a procedure. arg's must be local variables. Nesting and recursion allowed. |
| **EXIT** | Leaves the procedure |
| **FOR** `select_statement` **DO** `compound_statement` | Executes "compound_statement" for every line that is returned by the SELECT statement |
| **IF** (condition) **THEN** `compound_statement` **[ELSE** `compound_statement]` | IF statement |
| **POST_EVENT** `name` | Posts the specified event |
| **SUSPEND** | Only for SELECT procedures which return tables: Waits for the client to request the next line. Returns the next line to the client. |
| **WHILE** (condition) **DO** `compound_statement` | WHILE statement. |
| **WHEN {EXCEPTION** a \| | Exception handling. WHEN statements must be at the end |

218

| | |
|---|---|
| `SQLCODE x | ANY} DO`<br><br>`compound_statement` | of the procedure, directly before the final END. |
| **EXECUTE STATEMENT**<br>`stringvalue` | Executes the DML statement in stringvalue |
| **EXECUTE STATEMENT**<br>`stringvalue`<br><br>**INTO** `variable_list` | Executes Statement and returns variables (singleton) |
| **FOR EXECUTE**<br>**STATEMENT**<br>`stringvalue`<br><br>**INTO** `variable_list`<br>**DO**<br>`compound_statement` | Executes Statement and iterates through the resulting lines |
| **EXECUTE STATEMENT**<br>`stringvalue` | Executes the DML statement in stringvalue |
| **EXECUTE STATEMENT**<br>`stringvalue`<br><br>**INTO** `variable_list` | Executes Statement and returns variables (singleton) |
| **FOR EXECUTE**<br>**STATEMENT**<br>`stringvalue`<br><br>**INTO** `variable_list`<br>**DO**<br>`compound_statement` | Executes Statement and iterates through the resulting lines |

**d i y** *Things to try...*

1/ Re-Write any one of the stored procedures as a stored function.

# 24  Using Cursors

In the previous chapter we briefly touched on cursors in one of the examples. In this chapter we are going to delve deeper into our discussion on cursors and how to use them.

In all the previous chapters we have used the SELECT statement to retrieve either all the resulting data or none. However there are times when you would need to step through the data one record at a time or simply move to the next or previous record at will.

This is where cursors come into their own. Cursors are usually used by interactive applications in which the user needs to scroll back and forth through data on their screen, browsing or making changes.

### *Using Cursors...*

Before you can use cursors in Firebird you need to perform a number of steps:

- Cursors must be declared. This simply defines the SELECT statement to be used. As we did in the previous chapter, that is, we defined CUR or Cursor for (select name from student).

- Once the cursor is declared, we can retrieve the data by opening the cursor. Issuing an open command, the cursor is populated with data from the SELECT statement assigned to it.

- Individual rows can now be retrieved (fetched) as needed.

- Once you have finished with the cursor you must close it.

Once a cursor has been declared it can be opened and closed as often as you like. You can fetch rows as often as needed also, once opened.

### Creating Cursors in Firebird...

To create a cursor we will declare it within a stored procedure.

In Firebird the syntax is as follows:

> DECLARE [VARIABLE] <cursor_name> CURSOR FOR
> (<select_statement>);

where

> cursor_name = The name of the cursor variable. The rules for declaring local variables in PSQL apply to it.
>
> select_statement = SELECT statement.

The CURSOR FOR statement is used to assign the select statement to the cursor_name variable.

Summary of the four steps mentioned above related to the four PSQL statements are as follows:

| | Command | Description |
|---|---|---|
| 1 | DECLARE CURSOR | Declares the cursor. The SELECT statement defines the data set returned for the cursor. |
| 2 | OPEN | Opens the data set for serial unidirectional access. |
| 3 | FETCH | Returns the current row from the current data set, starting with the first line. |
| 4 | CLOSE | Closes the cursor and releases system resources. |

Let us create the stored procedure GetStudentNames

222

Type and execute the following example:

```
SQL> SET TERM !! ;
SQL> CREATE OR ALTER PROCEDURE GetStudentNames
CON> RETURNS (
CON> SNAME CHAR (20)
CON> ) AS
CON> DECLARE CUR CURSOR FOR (SELECT NAME FROM STUDENT);
CON> BEGIN
CON> OPEN CUR;
CON> WHILE (1=1) DO
CON> BEGIN
CON> FETCH CUR INTO :SNAME;
CON> IF (ROW_COUNT = 0) THEN
CON> LEAVE;
CON> SUSPEND;
CON> END
CON> CLOSE CUR;
CON> END !!
SQL> SET TERM ; !!
```

Now execute the procedure by typing and executing the following:

```
SQL> EXECUTE PROCEDURE GETSTUDENTNAMES;
```

You should get a single row returned as follows.

```
SNAME
====================
John smith
```

But we know that the student table has more that one student record. This is because this stored procedure is called a 'selectable procedure', i.e. the SUSPEND command, when execution of a PSQL routine continues until the next value is requested by the calling application, and returns output values, if any, to the calling application.

When the procedure is called from an EXECUTE PROCEDURE statement, then SUSPEND has the same effect as EXIT. This usage is legal, but not recommended.

223

Therefore if we want to see the list we need to call the stored procedure from within a SELECT statement.

ⓘ The cursor is a one-way pointer to an ordered set of data returned by a SELECT expression in the DECLARE CURSOR statement, which allows you to obtain consistent, unidirectional access to the returned data.

Type and execute the following:

```
SQL> SELECT * FROM GETSTUDENTNAMES;
```

You should now get the following results:

```
SNAME
====================
John smith
Peter Hollis
Mathew Syed
Fiona Jones
Jane Headly
James Brown

SQL>
```

Let us take a closer look at our GetStudentNames procedure.

```
1.  SET TERM !! ;
2.  CREATE OR ALTER PROCEDURE GetStudentNames
3.  RETURNS (
4.  SNAME CHAR (20)
5.  ) AS
6.  DECLARE CUR CURSOR FOR (SELECT NAME FROM STUDENT);
7.  BEGIN
8.    OPEN CUR;
9.    WHILE (1=1) DO
10.   BEGIN
11.     FETCH CUR INTO :SNAME;
12.     IF (ROW_COUNT = 0) THEN
13.       LEAVE;
14.     SUSPEND;
```

```
15.    END
16.    CLOSE CUR;
17.    END !!
18. SET TERM ; !!
```

Line 1 and 18 we dealt with in the previous chapter.

Line 2 allows you to either create a new stored procedure or alter it, if it already exists.

Line 3,4 and 5 allow us to declare the variables we wish to return, in this case SNAME will hold and output the retrieved name from the student table fetched.

Line 6 is where we declare our cursor CUR and assign it to our select statement. The declaration does not actually retrieve any data. It simply defines the select statement to be used.

Line 8 is where we OPEN and retrieve data into our cursor CUR.

Lines 9 to 15 is our WHILE *loop* block.

Line 11, the first time in the while loop, we fetch the first data row from cur.

Line 12 we perform a quick test to see if there are no rows of data in the select query the cur points to.

If ROW_COUNT is zero then LEAVE (EXIT can also be used) the while loop.

Line 14 SUSPEND or wait for the calling program to respond that the FETCH was successful.

Then move the cur to the next record waiting for the next FETCH. Once the CUR reaches the end, ROW_COUNT will be zero then the *whileloop* is exited and the cursor is CLOSED on line 16 and the program ends in line 17.

We will end our discussion on Cursors here.

In the next chapter we will turn our attention to using triggers in Firebird.

# 25  Using Triggers

We have seen so far that stored procedures/functions as well as SQL statements in Firebird are executed when they are needed, but what if we want a procedure or statement to be executed (triggered) automatically when an events occurs? For example:

- Whenever a student adds his/her email to check that the format is correct.

- Whenever a library book is loaned to a student or staff, to update automatically the quantity left and the days on loan.

- When a payment towards their debt is paid, to update their account balance.

These all need to be processed automatically. Somehow the system needs to know when these events occur and then perform some actions. And that is where 'triggers' come into the picture.

In Firebird a trigger is a self-contained module that executes automatically when an event occurs.

Triggers are similar to stored procedures and are created in similar ways. However triggers differ in that triggers:

- cannot be 'called' by applications or other procedures.

- cannot take inputs or pass outputs.

- PSQL includes certain extensions applicable only to trigger modules.

Triggers are mainly used to respond to statements that either DELETE, INSERT or UPDATE data.

Therefore Firebird triggers execute at row level, every time a row changes.

Firebird does support a certain degree of granularity for defining the timing, sequence, and conditions under which a particular trigger module will fire.

## Phase, Event, and Sequence...

A trigger can be called in one of two phases, either before data is written to a table or after data is written to a table. This, as stated above, can respond to one of three events i.e. deletions, insertions or updates.

When it comes to sequencing, Firebird allows multiple trigger modules for each phase/event combination. This can be as many as you need (within reasonable scope). Best practice is to use sequence numbers to set the order of executions from zero to (n). Numbers do not have to be unique and there can be gaps in your numbering.

## Creating Triggers...

Triggers are created with the CREATE TRIGGER statement. When creating a trigger you need to specify four pieces of information.

- A trigger name that is unique within the database.

- A table name that associates the table with the trigger.

- The action that determines the state, phase/event, and optional sequence that the trigger should respond to (DELETE, INSERT, or UPDATE).

- When the trigger should be executed (before or after processing).

Syntax

```
CREATE TRIGGER name
   {<relation_trigger_legacy>
      | <relation_trigger_sql2003>
      | <database_trigger>          }
   AS
      [<declarations>]
BEGIN
      [<statements>]
END
```

We will be using our Looptest table in the following example to demonstrate Firebird triggers.
In this example we will let a trigger populate the id column automatically.

In order for us to do this, we need to perform a few steps first:

- We need to find what the current id number is.

- We need to setup some sort of sequence generator.

- Attach it to our trigger.

Let us start with our second point. The setting up of a sequence generator. Fortunately Firebird has such a mechanism. This will be a two-set operation:

- first we need to create a generator, then we set its value to the next number in the sequence.

From the isql prompt type the following:

```
SQL> CREATE GENERATOR Looptest_id;
SQL>
```

This will create the generator Looptest_id;

Now we need to determine the max id number and we do this as follows:

```
SQL> select Max(id) from looptest;

     MAX
=============
      6
```

In this example the max number is 6

Therefore we need to set our generator to '7' as follows

```
SQL> SET GENERATOR Looptest_id TO 7;
```

Type the following:

SET TERM ; !!

```
SQL>
SQL> CREATE TRIGGER Create_looptestid FOR looptest
CON> BEFORE INSERT
CON> AS BEGIN
CON> NEW.ID = GEN_ID(Looptest_id,1);
CON> END !!
```

SET TERM !! ;

Now before we insert some data into our looptest table let us see what we have so far:

Type the following:

Select * from looptest;

You should have something similar for the screen shown below:

```
SQL> select * from looptest;
         ID NAME

=============== ==================
============
          1 John smith

          2 Peter Hollis

          3 Mathew Syed

          4 Fiona Jones

          5 Jane Headly

          6 James Brown
```

Now let's insert a name into the looptest table. Type the following:

```
SQL> INSERT INTO LOOPTEST (NAME) VALUES ('Fred Bloggs');
SQL>
```

Now, if you re-run Select * from looptest; you should see that our automatic sequence starts at '8' in this example.

```
SQL>
SQL> select * from looptest;
        ID  NAME

============  ================
============
         8  Fred Bloggs

         1  John smith

         2  Peter Hollis

         3  Mathew Syed

         4  Fiona Jones

         5  Jane Headly

         6  James Brown
```

Insert a few more names to see what you get.

Now let us take a look at our trigger:

```
SQL>
SQL> CREATE TRIGGER Create_looptestid FOR looptest
CON> BEFORE INSERT
CON> AS BEGIN
CON> NEW.ID = GEN_ID(Looptest_id,1);
CON> END !!
SQL>
```

Notice the line BEFORE INSERT this tells Firebird to execute (fire) trigger before data is written to the table. If we wanted the trigger to be fired after insert we would simply write AFTER INSERT.

Also notice the NEW.ID line GEN_ID calls our generator and increments it by one in our case, e.g. GEN_ID (Looptest_id,1). Therefore, instead of returning '7 ' for our initial first call, instead we set our generator to '7' knowing it will create a gap in our sequence.

Sometimes it is necessary to do this for a number of reasons. If you are performing a very big migration from one system to another, you may want to start your block from a new start position from the old data block. For example, you may have purchased or taken over a GP practice and wish to add your predecessor's data to your system. Again you may start your block from say 5000 where your precedecessor's data ended at, say, 3456.

Note that if you wanted to trigger an event on both an action which inserts or updates data, then you can simply type:

BEFORE INSERT OR UPDATE

For firing a trigger on a delete action, we simply replace INSERT with DELETE.

Trigger can also be altered so instead of writing CREATE we could write ALTER TRIGGER...

It is common (and recommended) that when creating triggers you write as follows:

CREATE OR ALTER TRIGGER....
In that way, if it does not exist it is created and if it exists, it can be altered.
You could also use the RECREATE Trigger command.

Firebird uses Creates or Recreates to create triggers.

If a trigger with the same name already exists, RECREATE TRIGGER will try to drop it and create a new trigger. RECREATE TRIGGER will fail if the existing trigger is in use.

When you no longer need a trigger you can delete it by issuing a DROP TRIGGER <triggername>; command.

The same goes for Generators if you no longer require a generator you can simply delete it as follows:

DROP GENERATOR <name>;

### *The final word on triggers*

Triggers in Firebird, as you can see, are fairly well supported. Although we have only briefly looked at triggers, you can see how effective they can be.

# 26  Transaction Processing

*What is Transaction Processing?...*

In chapter 18 we looked at how we can maintain some basic referential integrity in our joined tables when updating or deleting data across our tables.

But how would we maintain the integrity of our data due to some sort of system failure? For example, a student wishes to pay a fine for late returned book and the system crashes, mid transaction.

Now, if the crash occurred while you were bringing up the student's record then this would not be a problem. However, what if the crash occurred mid-way in recording the fine? The system will be left with a partial transaction hanging around in the system. How do we ensure that this does not happen (or at least minimize the risk)? This is where transaction processing comes in.

Transaction processing is used to maintain database integrity by ensuring that batches of Firebird SQL operations execute either completely or not at all. There is never any partial completion.

Now, lets re-examine our example with the use of transaction operations. This is how the process would work:
Assume we had a BookLoan and a BookFine table and a relationship link between them.

The student has brought the book back late and therefore the student fine is calculated as:

Fine = dayrate (£0.15) x Number of days late.

The process involved could be:
- Retrieve the Student's information
- Retrieve the Student Code.

- Check the student BookLoan balance.
- Add calculated balance and Update BookLoan
- If a failure occurs while updating the row, then roll back (undo) action.
- Retrieve BookLoan ID
- Add a row to the BookFine table and add amount paid.
- If a failure occurs while adding the row, then roll back (undo) action.
- Update BookLoan balance.
- If a failure occurs while adding the row, then roll back (undo) action.
- Commit the BookLoan payment information.

When working with transaction processing Firebird provides the following operators:

SET TRANSACTION: for configuring and starting a transaction
COMMIT: to signal the end of a unit of work and write changes permanently to the database
ROLLBACK: to reverse the changes performed in the transaction
SAVEPOINT: to mark a position in the log of work done, in case a partial rollback is needed
RELEASE SAVEPOINT: to erase a savepoint

*Managing Transactions...*

The key to managing transactions involves breaking your SQL statements into logical sections and explicitly stating where data should be rolled back and when not to roll back.

As mentioned above Firebird uses the SET TRANSACTION statement to configure and start a transaction.

*Using ROLLBACK...*

The Firebird *ROLLBACK* command is used to roll back (undo) Firebird statements.

Consider the following example:

```
SELECT * FROM looptest;
SET TRANSACTION;
DELETE FROM looptest;
SELECT * FROM looptest;
ROLLBACK;
SELECT * FROM looptest;
```

The result from executing the above batch statements is as follows:

| | 123 ID | ABC NAME |
|---|---|---|
| 1 | 8 | Fred Bloggs |
| 2 | 9 | Jasmine Baker |
| 3 | 1 | John smith |
| 4 | 2 | Peter Hollis |
| 5 | 3 | Mathew Syed |
| 6 | 4 | Fiona Jones |
| 7 | 5 | Jane Headly |
| 8 | 6 | James Brown |

Now, without marking the start of where we wish to monitor the transaction, and without rolling (undoing) our statement and then Looptest table on the final SELECT statement, we would have returned an empty resultant record set.

This example begins by displaying the contents of the Looptest table. By issuing a SELECT statement we then start a transaction and delete all the contents of the Looptest table.

We perform another SELECT to verify that the content has been deleted.
We then undo or roll-back these deleted records, and perform another SELECT to verify that the deleted records have been restored.

(i) Note, ROLLBACK can only be used after a SET TRANSACTION statement has been executed.

It is worth noting here also, that transaction processing is used to manage INSERT, UPDATE AND DELETE statements. You cannot ROLLBACK CREATE or DROP operations.

### Using COMMIT...

Firebird SQL statements are usually executed and written directly to the database table. This is known as *implicit commit,* that is, it writes and saves changes immediately. These operations happen automatically.

When working with transactions, *commits* do not occur automatically (implicitly). For your transactions to be written and saved to the table you have to <u>explicitly</u> force the commitment.

This is done with Firebird's COMMIT statement.

(i) It should be noted, when considering portability if you decide to port your data to another RDBMS, that not all RDBMSs support *Transaction* functions (i.e.

explicit operations), even if they have an auto commit on/off flag. Therefore, always check first, before you commit (*no pun intended*) to another RDBMS.

Now Type and execute the following:

```
CREATE TABLE LOOPTEST2 (
        ID INTEGER DEFAULT NULL,
        NAME CHAR(150) DEFAULT NULL
) ;
```

We will now use *Transaction* to populate the LOOPTEST2 table.

Now Type and execute the following:

```
SELECT * FROM LOOPTEST2;
SET TRANSACTION;
INSERT INTO LOOPTEST2 (ID, NAME) SELECT * FROM
LOOPTEST;
SELECT * FROM LOOPTEST2;
```

Notice the result from the final SELECT statement is blank:

We have not yet committed the changes.

Now add the COMMIT statement and perform another select as follows:

```
SELECT * FROM LOOPTEST2;
SET TRANSACTION;
INSERT INTO LOOPTEST2 (ID, NAME) SELECT * FROM
LOOPTEST;
SELECT * FROM LOOPTEST2;
COMMIT;
```

```
SELECT * FROM LOOPTEST2;
```
Now you should get a similar result, as shown below:

| | 123 ID | ABC NAME |
|---|---|---|
| 1 | 8 | Fred Bloggs |
| 2 | 9 | Jasmine Baker |
| 3 | 1 | John smith |
| 4 | 2 | Peter Hollis |
| 5 | 3 | Mathew Syed |
| 6 | 4 | Fiona Jones |
| 7 | 5 | Jane Headly |
| 8 | 6 | James Brown |

ⓘ *(if DBeaver reports an error, you may need to exit and restart DBeaver because the set transaction block is waiting for an end statement it commit or rollback).*

Here you will see that once we have forced the write and save, the data is now recorded in the LOOPTEST2 table, we verified this with a final select statement.

### Using SAVEPOINT...

Our transaction examples so far have been simple transactions where the entire transaction can be rolled back. However for more complex transactions undoing the entire transaction may not be desirable. Therefore we may need partial commit or rollback. This is where SAVEPOINT comes in.

Firebird supports rollback of partial transactions by allowing you to strategically put place-holders at various locations within your transaction block. These placeholders are referred to as *savepoints*.

To create a *savepoint* within your transaction block you simply use the command SAVEPOINT within your transaction SQL statement.

Each savepoint is assigned a unique name so that if a rollback is necessary, you can specify where to rollback to.

Syntax
        SAVEPOINT sp_name

example,

SAVEPOINT delete_A;
        ….
        ….
ROLLBACK TO delete_A;


### *Overriding Firebird's default Commit behaviour...*

By default Firebird automatically *commits* any and all changes. In other words, when you execute a Firebird SQL statement, the changes are made immediately against the table. However, you can instruct Firebird to not commit changes automatically. You do this by issuing the following statement: **SET AUTODDL OFF;** conversely, if you wish to turn back on an automatic *commit* then you would issue the following: **SET AUTODDL ON;**

### *Understanding Firebird Transactions...*

We have had a brief look at transactions. However, as the transaction function is considered the cornerstone of RDBMSs, it is only right that we lift the bonnet and take a closer look at how Firebird controls transactions. By understanding how Firebird implements transactions it will help your understanding about diagnosing performance issues and enhance the process of developing applications when using Firebird RDBMS.

It is worth noting that every RDBMS will implement transactions differently. Therefore understanding their particular methods of implementation should aid in a more robust application.

*Basic requirements for transaction processing...*

The basic requirements for maintaining integrity in a database can be summarized in four basic requirements that any respectable RDBMS must meet. These are Atomicity, Consistency, Isolation and Durability (often referred by their acronym as ACID requirements).

### Atomicity
As previously stated, atomicity requires that each transaction be "all or nothing": if one part of the transaction fails, then the entire transaction fails, and the database state is left unchanged. An atomic system must guarantee atomicity in each and every situation, including power failures, errors and crashes. To the outside world, a *committed* transaction appears (by its effects on the database) to be indivisible ("atomic"), and an aborted transaction does not happen. All data-transforming operations performed within single transaction are realised as a single indivisible operation.

### Consistency
The aim here is to ensure that any transaction will bring the database from one valid state to another. Any data written to the database must be valid according to all defined rules, including constraints, cascades, triggers, and any combination thereof. This does not guarantee correctness of the transaction in all the ways the application programmer might have wanted (that is the responsibility of application-level code), but merely that any programming errors cannot result in the violation of any defined rules. It should be noted that the database could be in an inconsistent state while running a transaction, but the final database state must be consistent.

### Isolation

All concurrent running transactions must be run in isolation from each other. Concurrency control is the main goal of isolation. Therefore any transient data transformations are not exposed to other transactions before the transaction completes.

### Durability

Once the data has been *committed*, then it is made <u>permanent</u> even after the power is lost and restored, the changes must remain.

On first reflection you would be correct to think ACID requirements are obvious. However how each RDBMS provider implements these requirements is quite another thing all together, and Firebird is no exception.

### Atomicity Strategy…

When it come to atomicity, almost all database systems write all the changes immediately to the database, along with information necessary for the database to restore itself to a previous state.

However when it comes down to it there are basically two implementation strategies used by most RDBMS providers.

### Strategy one

This approach only the latest data  contained in the database, and therefore updates, deletions and insert is only on the latest data. For recovery to the previous data a separate file is stored from the database, which contains recovery information. This file is usually called the 'transaction log'.

The most common implications of this approach are:

- Rollback can be an expensive operation, not to mention very time consuming.
- The risk of rolling back not only partial transactions but also *committed* ones can occur.

- Because the Transaction log is stored separate from the database, it is relatively easy to archive or delete outdated recovery data logs.
- Incremental backups are easy to implement.
- Because multiple concurrent Transactions need to use the Transaction log file, it becomes most important that good strict Isolation (lock/unlock mechanism) is implemented.

### Strategy two

With this approach the database can contain multiple versions of data rows, so any row that is going to be updated is left intact, and a new row version is created instead of a direct row update.

This strategy is also known as Multi-Generational Architecture (MGA). This is the strategy that Firebird uses, and it was first used by InterBase (Firebird's predecessor).

The most common implication of this approach are:

- Rollback is relatively inexpensive.
- Recovery information is stored directly in the database. However some management of the archiving of old data is needed to aid in performance.
- With this strategy the database will contain multiple states of data, therefore the implementation of Isolation strategy will be different to the strategy that uses the single transaction log file.

Therefore when developing a Firebird application the MGA strategy is the one to be considered.

### Consistency Strategy...

The consistency of the data integrity depends on the RDBMS and you, the developer. We have already come across referential integrity, the RDBMS most likely will support such things as data validation constraints, triggers and stored procedures, etc.

Remember, not all RDBMSs will come with the same built-in consistency constraint support. Therefore understanding Firebird's in-built support will aid in your application development.

### Isolation Strategy...

Isolation strategies are considered very complicated, and is beyond the scope of this book to delve deeply into. But it pays to have some knowledge of the strategies, especially in regards to Firebird. The purpose of isolation strategy is to prevent interference between concurrent transactions that would lead to data loss or incorrect data interpretation or calculations.

Briefly these are:

*Lost Updates*. If two users are seeing the same view of the data and one makes changes almost immediately after the first user made changes, then Lost updates are likely to occur.

### Dirty reads
A dirty read (also called uncommitted dependency) occurs when a transaction is allowed to read data from a row that has been modified by another running transaction and not yet *committed*.

### Non-repeatable read
A non-repeatable read is one in which data read twice inside the same transaction cannot be guaranteed to contain the same value. Depending on the isolation level, another transaction could have nipped in and updated the value between the two reads. Non-repeatable reads occur, because at lower isolation levels, reading data only locks the data for the duration of the read, rather than for the duration of the transaction. Sometimes this behaviour might be completely desirable. Some applications may want to know the absolute, real-time value, even mid transaction, whereas other types of transactions might need to read the same value multiple times.

*Phantom rows*
Which arise when one user can select some but not all the new rows written by another user. New rows can be added by other transactions, so you get a different number of rows by firing the same query in the current transaction. In REPEATABLE READ isolation levels Shared locks are acquired.

*Interleaved transactions.* These can arise when changes in one row by one user affects the data in other rows in the same table or in other tables being accessed by other users. They are usually timing-related, occurring when there is no way to control or predict the sequence in which users perform the changes.

To prevent these issues, the database system must:

- Protect all data read by a transaction from changes by other transactions.
- Ensure that data read by a transaction can also be changed by this transaction.
- Ensure that pending changes made by a transaction will not be accessible to other transactions. Which can be translated into a single general requirement that: a write operation from one transaction must be mutually exclusive with any other operation (including read) on the same data from other transactions.

Firebird uses locks as most databases do. However Firebird and any RDBMS that uses MGA uses locks differently from those that use transaction log files.

Firebird databases don't need to protect readers by "locking" all attempts to write from other transactions, because the old data values are still present in the database as old row versions, and are thus available for readers. Firebird databases also don't need separate locks to protect writes from overwriting, because this requirement can be determined from the existence of row versions.

Firebird databases need to use locks only in special cases that cannot be resolved in another way (e.g. when it is necessary to ensure that data, once read, could also be updated). Therefore Firebird and any RDBMS that supports MGA has better potential to provide higher concurrency, but both architectures have a basic problem with data access serialisation if they fulfil the general requirement that a write operation from one transaction must be mutually exclusive with any operation on the same data from other transactions.

Moving the serialisation down from database level to row, database page or table level, can reduce contention between transactions if they operate in different parts of database, but it also creates room for deadlocks.

The solution to this is far from perfect: the best we can do is devise some sort of compromise between data consistency and concurrency, which is in fact what most RDBMSs do.

### Durability Strategy...

As mentioned previously, once the data has been *committed*, then it is made permanent even after the power is lost and restored, the changes must remain.

*In summing up the Implementation of transactions in Firebird*

Firebird implementation of transactions, is built on:

- The creation of versions (record version) for each data record (table row). These record versions are stored in database as a linked list for each row, where the most recent record version maintains a constant position in the database. Each record version contains an identification number of the transaction that created it, and a pointer to its previous record version. A new record version is also created for deleted rows, but it's a very small one that indicates the deleted row.

- Bookkeeping of transaction states. Transaction states are stored as a bitmap indexed by transaction number, where each transaction state is encoded with two bits. To minimise memory consumption, this table doesn't hold states for all transactions, but it's reduced only to the range of transaction numbers starting from the oldest (with smallest transaction number) uncommitted transaction (the so called Oldest Interesting Transaction - OIT) to the most recent transaction.
- Tracking of "important" transaction numbers. Firebird transaction numbers for Next Transaction, Oldest Interesting Transaction (see above) and Oldest Active Transaction (OAT) are stored in the database in the Database Header Page, and are recalculated and written whenever a new transaction is started.

We will end our brief discussion here. Understanding the underpinning implementation of Firebird's transaction strategy will greatly improve your ability to deliver robust, stable database applications.

# 27 Understanding Globalization and Localization

Firebird is used throughout the world, and as such it needs to accommodate different languages, different alphanumeric characters set as well as different ways to sort and retrieve data.

When developing applications that require multilingual database features, you will have to take into consideration such things as the character set to use, the letters and symbols. Sounds simple if you only have one language to consider. But when your application will be used in multiple countries for example France with characters such as é or German the Ö, and to complicate matters more, non-Latin based character sets may need to be considered, for example (Japanese, Hebrew, Russian, Arabic, etc.)

Other considerations to take into account would be 'encodings' I.e. how character sets are represented internally.

When looking at how characters are to be compared then collation consideration becomes quite important when handling multilingual character sets.

For example consider if you want your database to sort by forename. Now consider the name John. It could be written JOHN, john, John. Now, is your database setup to be case-insensitive or case-sensitive? And this is only in consideration for an English character set. As mentioned above, the complexity increases with different language sets.

### Confusion between UNICODE and UTF-x...

As you can imagine a need for some sort of standardizing is needed. Earlier attempts to standardized have been made such as ACSII, and ISO/IEC 8859 is a joint ISO and IEC series of standards for 8-bit character encoding. However, as character sets grow both standardized system's limitations became obvious.

This gave birth to the Unicode. The Unicode was developed to go beyond the limitation of the ISO/IEC 8859 character encoding set. Now you may have heard the term Unicode and UTF-x where x can represent 8, 16, 32 and several other numbers.

This has led to confusion amongst programmers and DB Administrators.

When computers first came on the scene they were limited to 8-bits, therefore it was common practice to only have one language character loaded at any one time. It was possible to map most language character sets using 8-bit, i.e. 7-bit for say English 0 to 127 and the additional 8$^{th}$ digit to extend to 128 characters for non-English characters.

However when you need to represent characters from more than one language, it would not be possible to cram them into a single byte (8 bits). Therefore a new encoding strategy is needed.

There are essentially two different types of encoding standards: one expands the value range by adding more bits. Examples of these encoding standards would be UCS2 (2 bytes = 16 bits) and UCS4 (4 bytes = 32 bits). They suffer from inherently the same problem as ASCII and ISO-8859 standards, as their value range is still limited, even if the limit is vastly higher.

The other encoding standard uses a variable number of bytes per character, and the most commonly known encoding standard for this is the Unicode Transformation Format or UTF (for short) encoding standard. All UTF encodings work in roughly the same manner: you choose a unit size, which for UTF-8 is 8 bits, for UTF-16 is 16 bits, and for UTF-32 is 32 bits. The standard then defines a few of these bits as flags: if they're set, then the next unit in a sequence of units is to be considered part of the same character. If they're not set, this unit represents one character fully. Thus the most common (English) characters only occupy one byte in UTF-8 (two in UTF-

16, 4 in UTF-32), but other language characters can occupy six bytes or more.

Both the UCS standards and the UTF standards encode the code points as defined in Unicode. In theory, those encodings could be used to encode any number.

Basically Unicode can be implemented by different character encodings such as UCS and UTF.

## UNICODE...

The Unicode Standard consists of a set of code charts for visual reference, an encoding method and a set of standard character encodings, a set of reference data files, and a number of related items, such as character properties, rules for normalization, decomposition, collation, rendering, and bidirectional display order (for the correct display of text containing both right-to-left scripts, such as Arabic and Hebrew, and left-to-right scripts).

ⓘ Unicode's success at unifying character sets has led to its widespread and predominant use in the internationalization and localization of computer software. The standard has been implemented in many recent technologies, including modern operating systems, XML, Java (and other programming languages), and the .NET Framework, along with most DBMSs including Firebird.

*Main advantages of using Unicode*

- One single Character Set for all languages/scripts
- No code overlaps
- Hardware and OS independent
- Standardization ISO 10646 goes beyond such standards as ASCII = ISO 646
- Started with 16 Bits/Character, now 32 Bits/Char
- Ability to code 1,114,112 characters, with over 137,000 code points defined so far
- Currently only a fraction is used

- Basic Multilingual Plane (BMP): 0..U+FFFF Can be encoded in 16 bits
- Current version: 11.0 (June 2018)
- Defines Characters, not Glyphs

### *Working with Firebird's Character Set and Collations...*

Every CHAR or VARCHAR column has a character set applied by Firebird.

In our student table

```
CREATE TABLE STUDENT (
CODE VARCHAR(20) DEFAULT NULL NOT NULL,
NAME CHAR(20) DEFAULT NULL,
....
....
```

However Firebird allows us to override the default:

For example type and execute the following:

```
create table persons (
        pers_id integer not null primary key,
        last_name char (150) character set utf8,
        first_name varchar (50) character set
        iso8859_1,
        middle_name varchar (50)
);
```

However the middle_name column will use the default character set.

Firebird also allows you the ability to set your own default character set for the whole databases for example:

```
CREATE DATABASE localhost:MyApp
  USER SYSDBA
  PASSWORD masterkey
```

```
PAGE_SIZE 4096
DEFAULT CHARACTER SET utf8;
```

## Collations...

Firebird from version 2.1 comes with UNICODE collations for all the standard character sets.

In order to be able to sort or compare strings, you also need to define a collation. A collation defines the sort ordering and uppercase conversions for a string.

Firebird is unable to transliterate between character sets. So you must set the correct values on the server and on the client if everything is to work correctly.

To create a collation type and execute the following:

```
create collation lat_uni
  for iso8859_1
from external ('ISO8859_1_UNICODE');
```

Now we need to populate our persons table and we can quickly do this as follows, using our Looptest table:

INSERT INTO persons (Pers_id, First_name) SELECT id, Name FROM looptest;

(i) Note some readers may find DBeaver does not perform this correctly. If this is the case simply use Firebird's isql utility.

```
SELECT Pers_id, first_name FROM persons
ORDER BY first_name COLLATE lat_uni;
```

```
      PERS_ID  FIRST_NAME
===========  =============
          4  Fiona Jones
          8  Fred Bloggs
          6  James Brown
          5  Jane Headly
          9  Jasmine Baker
          1  John smith
          3  Mathew Syed
          2  Peter Hollis
SQL>
```

We can now use SELECT to specify our alternate collation sequence. Consider the following example:

SELECT Pers_id, First_Name FROM persons
WHERE First_NAME COLLATE lat_uni like '%John smith%'
ORDER BY First_name;

When considering which character set to use, it may be worth considering such issues as:

- Whether the application will be used on different hardware platforms.

- Whether the application will be used on different Operating Systems.

- Whether you need to take into consideration multilingual requirements.

If you have responded "yes" to any of the above then it is recommended that you use Unicode.

You may recall in chapter 14, Text Manipulation, that when comparing text we found that text filtering was case-sensitive. One technique we used to handle this was to use the UPPERCASE function.

Using Unicode we are define casing rules for UPPER(), LOWER()

```
SELECT *
FROM Student
WHERE UPPER (NAME COLLATE DE_DE) = :SEARCHNAME
ORDER BY NAME COLLATE FR_CA
```

### *Best Practice when working with Multi Language database design...*

As you can imagine there may be many approaches to handling multi-language database design. However one approach that is quite commonly used is to create two tables for each multilingual object.

The first table contains only language-neutral data (primary key, etc.) and the second table contains one record per language, containing the localized data plus the ISO code of the language.

In some cases you could add a Default Language field, so that we can fall-back to that language if no localized data is available for a specified language.

For example:

```
Table "Course_Student":
-----------------
IDCODE                : varchar
<any other language-neutral fields>


Table "StudentTranslations"
---------------------------
IDCODE                : varchar (foreign key
referencing the Student
Language              : varchar  (e.g. "en-UK",
"de-DE")
IsDefault             : bit
ProductDescription : nvarchar
<any other localized data>
```

In this way, multiple languages can be handled, without the need to add additional fields for each new language.

We will end here with a final point worth noting. You can, if needs be, use the CAST to convert between character sets.

# 28  Managing Security

*Understanding Security and Access Control...*

Databases are used to store data. Much of the data stored in a database is considered 'sensitive' information such as personal identifiable or private.
Therefore, not everyone who has access to the database should be given access to every recorded function in the database. In other words, users should have access only to the data they need to help them carry out their task: no more or no less.

For example:

- Most users will need to read and write data to tables. But rarely will they need to create and delete tables.

- Some users will not be allowed to view their colleague's personal information such as bank details, date of birth, medical data, etc.

- You may want users to access data via stored procedures but never directly.

- You may grant users the ability to add data but never to delete.

- Some users you may grant the ability to view data only but never to add or change.

These are just a few examples. Most western countries enforce strict laws that hold companies accountable for the data they hold and the secure management they have in place.

The procedures to manage your users access levels is called *access control.*

In Firebird you logged on with the Administrator level access. Administrator access gives a user maximum access to everything within the database environment. Obviously, no-one except the Database Administrator should have this level of control.

The Administrator uses administrative functions within the database, as the title suggests. This account user will be responsible for setting up and managing user level access. In Firebird the user is *SYSDBA* by default with the default password *masterkey* (you first came across this in chapter 2).

Throughout this book we used the Administrator user (*or superuser as it is sometimes called*) and that is fine, however in the real world you should never login as administrator to carry out a routine task.

Basic practice is to create a series of accounts for various user groups, some for Admin tasks, some for end-users, some for developers, etc.

ⓘ Note: Avoid using the SYSDBA user where possible, because this user role is considered sacred (superuser access level).

### Managing Users in Firebird...

Firebird has the RDB$ADMIN system role, which is predefined in every database. Granting someone the RDB$ADMIN role in a database gives him or her SYSDBA rights in that database only. In a normal database, this means full control over all objects. In the security database, it means the ability to create, alter and drop user accounts. In both cases, the grantee can always pass the role on to others. In other words, "WITH ADMIN OPTION" is built in and need not be specified.

### Granting the RDB$ADMIN role in the security database...

In a regular database, the RDB$ADMIN role can be granted and revoked with the usual syntax:

```
GRANT RDB$ADMIN TO username
REVOKE RDB$ADMIN FROM username
```

## In the security database

### Granting the RDB$ADMIN role in the security database

Since nobody can connect to the security database, the
GRANT and REVOKE statements cannot be used here.
Instead, the RDB$ADMIN role is granted and revoked with
the

SQL user management commands:

```
CREATE USER newuser PASSWORD 'password'
GRANT ADMIN ROLE
ALTER USER existinguser GRANT ADMIN
ROLE
ALTER USER existinguser REVOKE ADMIN
ROLE
```

Please notice that GRANT ADMIN ROLE and REVOKE
ADMIN ROLE are not GRANT and REVOKE statements.
They are three-word parameters to CREATE and ALTER
USER.

For now we will focus on how to create regular users (no admin
user privilege).

Using isql utility type the following:

SHOW USERS;

This will list the users currently in the database.

Now type the following:

SHOW GRANTS;

```
SQL> SHOW GRANTS;
There is no privilege granted in this database
SQL>
```

You should get a similar output as shown above.

### CREATE USER...

Syntax:

```
CREATE USER username PASSWORD 'password'
   [FIRSTNAME 'firstname']
   [MIDDLENAME 'middlename']
   [LASTNAME 'lastname']
   [GRANT ADMIN ROLE]
```

Type the following examples:

Now if you type SHOW USERS you should get a list of not just the SYSDBA and Staff user but also derick, jim and wendy.

Note that user wendy has been given the RDB$ADMIN role in the security database. This allows her to manage user accounts, but doesn't give her any special privileges in regular databases.

### ALTER USER...

```
SQL>
SQL> ALTER USER derick PASSWORD 'as!1Gwe' GRANT ADMIN ROLE;
SQL>
```

```
SQL>
SQL> CREATE USER derick PASSWORD 'as!1Gwe';
SQL> CREATE USER jim PASSWORD 'eciff03rb1L' FIRSTNAME 'Jimmy' LASTNAME 'Jones';
SQL> CREATE USER wendy PASSWORD 'F00tL00zE' FIRSTNAME 'Wendy' GRANT ADMIN ROLE;
SQL>
```

Now type and execute the following:

```
SQL>
SQL> GRANT RDB$ADMIN TO derick;
SQL>
```

This will grant derick access to the security database.

Type and execute the following to show grants created in the database:

```
SQL> SHOW GRANTS;

/* Grant permissions for this database */
GRANT RDB$ADMIN TO DERICK GRANTED BY SYSDBA
```

The resultant output should be as shown above.

### ROLES...

Rather than managing many individual privileges being granted and revoked repetitively and in an ad-hoc manor, Firebird supports an operation called 'roles'. A role is created in a database and is only available to that database. A role basically allows you to package a set of SQL privileges. Therefore these roles can now be assigned to a user. Note a role is granted ALL privileges or revokes ALL privileges, you cannot grant privileges in part.

#### CREATE ROLE...

To create a role we simply type

CREATE ROLE <rolename>;

for example CREATE ROLE manager;

#### GRANT PRIVILEGES...

When a privilege is granted, it is normally stored in the database with the current user as the granter. With the GRANTED BY clause, the user who grants the privilege can have someone else registered as the granter.

Consider the following examples

```
GRANT manager TO derick WITH ADMIN OPTION
GRANTED BY wendy;
```

This examples says GRANT manager to derick with admin option – all in wendy's name

therefore the syntax is:

GRANT

> {<privileges> ON <object> | role}
>   TO <grantees>
>   [WITH {GRANT|ADMIN} OPTION]
>   [{GRANTED BY | AS} [USER] granter]

Consider the following examples for granting privileges on tables.

```
GRANT SELECT, INSERT ON TABLE COURSE TO USER
jim;

GRANT SELECT ON TABLE STUDENT TO ROLE MANAGER,
USER derick;

GRANT ALL ON TABLE STUDENT TO ROLE MANAGER WITH
GRANT OPTION;

GRANT EXECUTE ON PROCEDURE WHILELOOP TO ROLE
MANAGER;
```

Privileges granted to tables can be INSERT, UPDATE, DELETE, SELECT, ALL, REFERENCES.

Also column names i.e. col,

### REVOKE...

As well as granting privileges you can also REVOKE privileges.

For examples

REVOKE ALL ON ALL FROM derick, wendy, jim;

### DELETING A USER,  ROLE...

To delete a user you simply type the following:

DROP USER <username>;

Therefore if you wanted to delete jim from the database you would type

DROP USER jim;

To also delete a role you simply type DROP ROLE <rolename>;

Therefore to delete the manager role you simply type:

DROP ROLE manager;

### In closing.

By no means has this chapter covered the  full subject of Firebird's security capability. To do so would be a complete book in itself. Hopefully the reader will be able to incorporate a fair level of security in their database applications. However I do recommend that you do further reading in this critical area of database management.

# 29  Firebird Database Maintenance and Housekeeping

*Backing Up and Restoring Firebird Database...*

You need to protect your business data. Data backup and data recovery are important parts of running a business. Business owners realize three things quickly: all computer systems crash; all humans make errors; and disasters happen when least expected or when you are least prepared for them. A business can be more prepared by having data backup systems in place.

Firebird comes with it's own backup and restore utility called GBAK.

GBAK is Firebird's command line tool for backup and restore of a complete database.

Most RDBMSs require that data is backed up regularly and Firebird is no different. Firebird being a disk-based files, meaning a normal copy and paste backup is possible. However this is NOT recommended.

There are graphical tools also available, however I would recommend you use the GBAK utility.

GBAK is able to perform a backup while the database is running (non-embedded mode only). There is no need to shut down the database during a GBAK backup. GBAK will create a consistent snapshot of the database at the time it starts running. You will, however, notice perfomance degradation during the backup, so it is a good idea to backup at night or during your quiet period. As GBAK visits all pages of the database, it will also perform garbage collection on the database.

*General Syntax*
gbak <options> -user <username> -password <password> <source> <destination>

## Backup

For backups, <source> is the database (= database string) you want to back up, <destination> is the path and file name of the backup file. The usual extension for the backup file is .fbk for Firebird.

Only SYSDBA or the database owner can perform a backup. For multi-file databases, specify only the name of the first file as the database name.

## Restore

For restores, <source> is the backup path file name and <destination> is the name of the database (= database string) that is to be built up from the backup file. You will have to specify the -C option for restore.

Let us take a look at gbak options:

At the command prompt (Linux console terminal) type and execute the following:

```
gbak -?
```

You should see a similar screen as the one shown below, listing all the possible flags and options you can use with the gbak utility.

```
C:\Users\dev2pc>gbak -?
gbak:Usage:
    gbak -b <db set> <backup set> [backup options] [general options]
    gbak -c <backup set> <db set> [restore options] [general options]
    <db set> = <database> | <db1 size1>...<dbN> (size in db pages)
    <backup set> = <backup> | <bk1 size1>...<bkN> (size in bytes = n[K|M|G])
    -recreate overwrite and -replace can be used instead of -c
gbak:legal switches are:
    -B(ACKUP_DATABASE)      backup database to file
    -C(REATE_DATABASE)      create database from backup file (restore)
    -R(ECREATE_DATABASE) [O(VERWRITE)] create (or replace if OVERWRITE used)
                            database from backup file (restore)
    -REP(LACE_DATABASE)     replace database from backup file (restore)
gbak:backup options are:
    -CO(NVERT)              backup external files as tables
    -E(XPAND)               no data compression
    -FA(CTOR)               blocking factor
    -G(ARBAGE_COLLECT)      inhibit garbage collection
    -IG(NORE)               ignore bad checksums
    -L(IMBO)                ignore transactions in limbo
    -NOD(BTRIGGERS)         do not run database triggers
    -NT                     Non-Transportable backup file format
    -OL(D_DESCRIPTIONS)     save old style metadata descriptions
    -T(RANSPORTABLE)        transportable backup -- data in XDR format
gbak:restore options are:
    -BU(FFERS)              override page buffers default
    -FIX_FSS_D(ATA)         fix malformed UNICODE_FSS data
    -FIX_FSS_M(ETADATA)     fix malformed UNICODE_FSS metadata
    -I(NACTIVE)             deactivate indexes during restore
    -K(ILL)                 restore without creating shadows
    -MO(DE) <access>        "read_only" or "read_write" access
    -N(O_VALIDITY)          do not restore database validity conditions
    -O(NE_AT_A_TIME)        restore one table at a time
    -P(AGE_SIZE)            override default page size
    -USE_(ALL_SPACE)        do not reserve space for record versions
gbak:general options are:
    -FE(TCH_PASSWORD)       fetch password from file
    -M(ETA_DATA)            backup or restore metadata only
    -PAS(SWORD)             Firebird password
    -RO(LE)                 Firebird SQL role
    -SE(RVICE)              use services manager
    -SKIP_D(ATA)            skip data for table
    -ST(ATISTICS) TDRW      show statistics:
       T                    time from start
       D                    delta time
       R                    page reads
       W                    page writes
    -TRU(STED)              use trusted authentication
    -USER                   Firebird user name
    -V(ERIFY)               report each action taken
    -VERBI(NT) <n>          verbose information with explicit interval
    -Y <path>               redirect/suppress status message output
    -Z                      print version number
gbak:switches can be abbreviated to the unparenthesized characters
```

Let us now perform a typical backup. Before you can perform a backup in our case you will need to close DBeaver (your application if you had one using the database. As only one app at a time can access our embedded database).

**Using Gbak…**

Now type and execute the following:

```
gbak -v -t -user SYSDBA -password "masterkey" c:\myapp\data\
MYAPP.FDB c:\myapp\data\myapp.fbk
```

You should see a screen full of the following:

```
gbak:    writing privilege for user SYSDBA
gbak:    writing privilege for user SYSDBA
gbak:    writing privilege for user SYSDBA
gbak:    writing privilege for user SYSDBA
gbak:    writing privilege for user SYSDBA
gbak:    writing privilege for user SYSDBA
gbak:    writing privilege for user SYSDBA
gbak:    writing privilege for user SYSDBA
```

ending:

```
gbak:writing security classes
gbak:writing table constraints
gbak:writing constraint INTEG_28
gbak:writing constraint INTEG_2
gbak:writing constraint PK_STUD
gbak:writing constraint INTEG_10
gbak:writing constraint PK_MYSTUD
gbak:writing constraint INTEG_48
gbak:writing constraint INTEG_49
gbak:writing constraint INTEG_33
gbak:writing constraint INTEG_66
gbak:writing constraint INTEG_34
gbak:writing constraint INTEG_67
gbak:writing constraint INTEG_29
gbak:writing constraint INTEG_30
gbak:writing constraint INTEG_41
gbak:writing referential constraints
gbak:writing check constraints
gbak:writing SQL roles
gbak:writing names mapping
gbak:closing file, committing, and finishing. 31744 bytes written
```

However you could replace -v -t with -b and that will simple backup quietly in the background.

*Restore*

There many be occasions where a restore is necessary. GBAK also allows us to perform a restore from the last backup (assuming we want the last backup data).

To perform a restore, type and execute the following:

266

Assuming we wish to replace our current database

```
gbak -REP -user SYSDBA -password masterkey c:\myapp\data\myapp.fbk
c:\myapp\data\MYAPP.FDB
```

However if you simply wish to restore by creating another duplicate then type and execute the following:

```
gbak -c -v -user SYSDBA -password masterkey c:\myapp\data\myapp.fbk
c:\myapp\data\MYAPP_dup.FDB
```

This is usually necessary if you want to extract a specific piece of information.

If you have not done so already, go to the folder of your database. e.g.

c:\myapp\data\

look at the .fdb file size and compare it to our backup .fbk.

Notice that our backup database size has significantly reduced in our case from about 2 mb to about 30kb. The backup is also compressed.

For further information on gbak then please visit:-
https://www.firebirdsql.org/pdfmanual/html/gbak.html


## Incremental backup.

It is not possible to perform an incremental backup with the GBAK utility. However Firebird also comes with nbackup utility that allows you to perform incremental backups.

With *nbackup* you can perform the following:

- Making and restoring of both full and incremental backups. An incremental backup only contains the mutations from your earlier full backup.

- Locking the main database file so you can subsequently back it up yourself with copying or backup tools of your own choice. In this mode, *nbackup* doesn't back up anything; it just creates the conditions under which you can safely make the backup yourself. Note, you can also use *nbackup* to restore a database.

Advantage of using *nbackup*

- Very Fast backup is possible because the database is written to the disk blindly.
- Because only incremental backups are performed this has a huge disk space saving potential.
- You can still compress the data (not as well as GBAK), backup, and restore with *nbackup*.

However, disadvantages of using *nbackup*

- *Nbackup* will not sweep and compact your database the way GBAK does.
- You can't change the database owner with an *nbackup* backup/restore cycle, like you can with GBAK.
- *Nbackup* can't make transportable backups, that is: backups you can restore on an incompatible platform or under another server version.

Take a look at the options for *nbackup*. Type and execute the following: *nbackup -?*

You should be presented with the following:

```
Physical Backup Manager    Copyright (C) 2004 Firebird development team
   Original idea is of Sean Leyne <sean@broadviewsoftware.com>
   Designed and implemented by Nickolay Samofatov <skidder@bssys.com>
   This work was funded through a grant from BroadView Software, Inc.

Usage: nbackup <options>
exclusive options are:
   -L(OCK) <database>                       Lock database for filesystem copy
   -UN(LOCK) <database>                     Unlock previously locked database
   -F(IXUP) <database>                      Fixup database after filesystem copy
   -B(ACKUP) <level> <db> [<file>]          Create incremental backup
   -R(ESTORE) <db> [<file0> [<file1>...]]   Restore incremental backup
special options are:
   -D(IRECT) [ON | OFF]                     Use or not direct I/O when backing up d
atabase
   -S(IZE)                                  Print database size in pages after lock

   -DE(COMPRESS) <command>                  Command to extract archives during rest
ore
general options are:
   -NOD(BTRIGGERS)                          Do not run database triggers
   -U(SER) <user>                           User name
   -RO(LE) <role>                           SQL role name
   -P(ASSWORD) <password>                   Password
   -FETCH_PASSWORD <file>                   Fetch password from file
   -Z                                       Print program version
switches can be abbreviated to the unparenthesized characters
Notes:
   <database> may specify database alias.
   Incremental backups of multi-file databases are not supported yet.
   "stdout" may be used as a value of <filename> for -B option.
   Option -S(IZE) only is valid together with -L(OCK).
   For historical reasons, -N is equivalent to -UN(LOCK)
   and -T is equivalent to -NOD(BTRIGGERS).
```

### Using nbackup...

If you decide to use *nbackup* for incremental backing up then your
first backup should be a full backup. We perform a full *nbackup*
(level 0) as follows:

```
nbackup -U SYSDBA -P masterkey -B 0 c:\myapp\data\myapp.fdb c:\
myapp\data\myapp_25-June-2018.nbk
```

```
c:\>nbackup -U SYSDBA -P masterkey -B 0 c:\myapp\data\myapp.fdb c:\myapp\data\my
app_25-June-2018.nbk
time elapsed     0 sec
page reads     264
page writes    264
```

-where '0' is the level backup and -'B'... you guessed correctly: it's
the Backup.

## Restore

```
nbackup -U SYSDBA -P masterkey -R c:\myapp\data\myapp.fdb c:\myapp\
data\myapp_25-June-2018.nbk
```

Note, the backup will fail if myapp.fdb already exists. In our given example, it will fail.

## Incremental backups

Assuming you will be performing backup on a daily basis then the next day you will do a level 1 backup.

Therefore type and execute the following:

```
nbackup -U SYSDBA -P masterkey -B 1 c:\myapp\data\myapp.fdb c:\
myapp\data\myapp_26-June-2018-1.nbk
```

```
c:\myapp\data>nbackup -U SYSDBA -P masterkey -B 1 c:\myapp\data\myapp.fdb c:\mya
pp\data\myapp_26-June-2018-1.nbk
time elapsed    0 sec
page reads      11
page writes     11
```

The following day would be:-

```
nbackup -U SYSDBA -P masterkey -B 2 c:\myapp\data\myapp.fdb c:\
myapp\data\myapp_26-June-2018-2.nbk
```

When performing a 'restore' operation, you will need to include all the backup files, therefore it is advisable not to have more than 4 to 5 incremental backups on rotation.

## Incremental restore from backups

syntax:

nbackup -R <database> [<backup0> [<backup1> [...]]]

270

For clarity (and to save you having to type the full path for each term in the list) navigate to the path of our database.

For Windows users type cd c:\myapp\data then hit enter-key

Now to perform a restore from incremental backup type and execute the following:

```
nbackup -R myapp2.fdb myapp_25-June-2018.nbk myapp_26-June-2018-
1.nbk myapp_26-June-2018-2.nbk
```

To avoid a file that already exist failure we will restore to myapp2.fdb database.

A final word on backups. Although there maybe many reasons why you will make backups, the most usual reason to backup is in the event that you or your company can no longer access the database, such as fire damage, theft,  or system failure..

In this case backups should be stored in a secure location and if possible off-site.

### *Corruptions...*

In an ideal world, systems never crash, everyone uses our perfect (!) system in a perfectly logical way. However back on the third rock from the sun (i.e. earth), things are not so perfect. Therefore we must plan for different eventualities. As well as backups, there may be rare occasions that the database becomes corrupted.  Firebird comes with a command-line utility that allows you to attempt to fix a damaged database called '*gfix*'.
Gfix allows attempts to fix corrupted databases, starting and stopping of databases, resolving any 'in limbo' transactions between multiple databases, changing the number of page buffers and so on. Gfix is a general purpose tool for system administrators (and database owners) to use that allows them to make various 'system level' changes to their databases.

Almost all the gfix commands have the same format when typed on the command line:

```
gfix [commands and parameters] database_name
```

The commands and their options are described in the following sections. The database name is the name of the primary database file which, for a single file database, is simply the database name and for multi-file databases. It is the first data file added.

### Shadow file handling...

A '*shadow*' is an exact, page-by-page copy of a database. Once a shadow is created, all changes made in the database are immediately reflected in the shadow. If the primary database file becomes unavailable for some reason, the DBMS will switch to the shadow.

More information on shadow file handling can be found here: https://firebirdsql.org/file/documentation/reference_manuals/fblangref25-en/html/fblangref25-ddl-shadow.html

More than one shadow file may exist for any given database and these may be activated and de-activated at will using the gfix utility.

### Garbage Collection...

Garbage Collection should be seen as an ongoing task of cleaning the database and is usually performed in the background. This constantly reorganizes the memory space used by the database. If you don't clean up, database performance will slowly (but surely) degrade.

Unwanted bits of data that Firebird leaves around is considered garbage (unwanted data), hence the name. This usually occurs after a transaction roll-back is being carried out. If you remember from our chapter on transaction, this is basically a copy of the row(s) from the table(s) that were being updated (or deleted) by the transaction prior to the rollback.

Because Firebird uses multi-generational architecture, every time a row is updated or deleted, Firebird keeps a copy in the database. These copies use space in the pages and can remain in the database for some time.

In addition to taking up space in the database, these old copies can lead to increased transaction startup times.

There are two types of garbage:

- Remnants from a committed transaction.

- Remnants from an aborted (rolled back) transaction.

These remnants are simply older copies of the rows that were being updated by the respective transactions. The differences are that:

- Whenever a subsequent transaction reaches garbage from a *committed* transaction, that garbage is automatically cleared out.

- Rolled back garbage is *never* automatically cleared out.

This means that on a database with a lot of rolled back transactions, there could be a large build-up of old copies of the rows that were updated and then rolled back.

Firebird will automatically sweep through the database and remove the remnants of rolled back transactions and this has two effects:

- The database size is reduced as the old copies of rows are deleted.

- The performance of the database may be affected while the sweep is in progress.

Automatic garbage collection for a new Firebird database has a sweep interval of 20,000msec The sweep interval is the *difference* between the *Oldest Snapshot Transaction,* or OST and the *Oldest Interesting Transaction* or OIT.

Note however, it will take place when the *difference* between the OST and the OIT is greater than the sweep interval, and therefore does not need to run every 20,000msec.

A manual garbage collection can run anytime by issuing the sweep command. The automatic sweep interval can be changed as follows:

> gfix -h[housekeeping] INTERVAL database_name

> for example

> gfix -h 5000 myapp

We will end our discussion of the Gfix utility here, and turn our attention to other maintainance tools that firebird has to offer.

However if you wish further information on gfix then I recommend you visit:

http://firebirdsql.org/pdfmanual/Firebird-gfix.pdf

### Firebird Log file...

Database log files are used extensively by DB administrators. Firebird maintains its log file named *"firebird.log"* The firebird.log file appears in the root of the Firebird installation in Windows installations. The firebird.log file appears in the /var/log sub-directory of the Firebird installation on Linux.

Take the time to understand the log file. Look for patterns, as the source of many problems often developed over a long period of time.

Some errors are not always immediately noticeable.

If you take a look at your log file you may see a typical entry as follows:

```
INET/inet_error: read errno = 10054
```

Error 10054 means that the user has disconnected. In our case you will see this each time you shutdown your application and therefore you can ignore this error.

Any procedures that fail will also be logged for example:

```
Deleting procedure WHILELOOP which is currently in use by
active user requests
```

Although not critical it simply means that this modifying procedure was called while others were using it. In our case DBeaver.

The log file is where you will identify such issues as page errors and possible corruptions, and page orphans. These are just a few of the likely errors that can be logged in the *firebird.log* file.

For a full description of all current 10xxx codes visit:-

http://www.firebirdfaq.org/faq119/

### Gstat – to analyze the Firebird database...

Another useful tool often used by administrators is the Gstat utility, which comes shipped with Firebird. This utility is used to analyze your Firebird database.

It is used to display statistical details about the contents of a database. Gstat does not connect to the database as other utilities do, instead it opens the database file(s) directly and reads through the raw data. Because of this, gstat is not transactionally aware and some of the statistics it gathers may include data that has been deleted, for example, by normal database transactions.

Gstat is normally called as follows:

```
gstat database_name [switches]
```

We can view Gstat by typing the following to your terminal screen:

gstag -?

```
C:\Users\dev2pc>gstat -?
usage:    gstat [options] <database> or gstat <database> [options]
Available switches:
      -a       analyze data and index pages
      -d       analyze data pages
      -e       analyze database encryption
      -h       analyze header page ONLY
      -i       analyze index leaf pages
      -s       analyze system relations in addition to user tables
      -u       username
      -p       password
      -fetch   fetch password from file
      -r       analyze average record and version length
      -t       tablename <tablename2...> <case sensitive>
      -role    SQL role name
      -tr      use trusted authentication
      -z       display version number
option -t accepts several table names only if used after <database>
```

For further information on how to use *gstat* visit:-

https://www.firebirdsql.org/pdfmanual/html/gstat.html

### *fbtracemgr...*

The Firebird Trace and Services API allows you to trace database and services events continuously.

The command-line tool *fbtracemgr* is included in the Firebird distribution, which exposes this feature to the end-user, although its feature set is limited in regards to taking full advantage of the Audit and Trace Services API in an user-friendly way. Using this utility will allow the user, to view raw traces of events.

The *fbtracemgr* is mainly useful where non-embedded firebird is used.

Type *fbtracemgr -?* to take a look at the various switches.

For further information on how to use *fbtracemgr* visit:-
https://www.upscene.com/documentation/fbtm2/index.html?
audit_and_trace_services_api.htm

### Firebird Services (fbsvcmgr)...

The utility *fbsvcmgr* provides a command-line interface to the
Services API, enabling access to any service that is implemented in
Firebird.

For further information on how to use *fbsvcmgr* visit:-
https://firebirdsql.org/rlsnotesh/rnfb210-util-svcs.html

# 30 Improving Performance and Administrative task

When it comes to performance you will find a large portion of your time will be spent on fine-tuning the performance of the database. Databases that perform sluggishly can usually be the result of a poorly implemented system of queries.

One of the first things we should consider when looking for ways to improve database performance is the type of hardware to use. When learning about Firebird DBMS or Application development using Firebird on an old PC (or your own PC) may be fine to use. However, for production ideally, this should be on a dedicated computer that meets the vendors hardware and operating system specifications.

Firebird comes pre-configured with default settings that are usually fine to begin with. But usually for production it is usual to tweak some of the settings or things such as the location of the temp file, disk space preallocation, memory allocation, to name just a few. These settings can be found in *firebird.conf* file.

Firebird comes with a number of tools that can help you to identify where possible performance issues maybe occurring.

### *Firebird Optimizer...*

The SQL language is designed to define requests for data manipulation, and to specify the final representation of results, but by design it does not support the definition of how the request should be handled by the database system. It's up to the database system to decide the best (i.e. fastest) method. This decision process is called optimization, and takes place as the last step of statement compilation. The part of the database engine responsible for statement optimization is called "the optimizer".

The purpose of the optimizer in Firebird is to decide:

- How relevant rows are selected, i.e. analyze, direct and indirect filter conditions.
- How data is read from the data stream (table, view, stored procedure). The access method could either be in storage order or out of storage order.
- Join order, if two or more data streams must be joined.
- How particular streams should be joined (Loop, Merge-sort or cross-product).

The optimizer uses various strategies to answer these questions. These include such things as join order, join methods, analyzing historic data, selection of relevant rows, etc.

The output from the optimizer is the final structure describing the joins to be made, and in which order they should be made.

The execution plan available through the isql commands SET PLAN or SET PLANONLY is simply a subset of the Record Selection Block (RSB) tree created by the optimizer, that has been converted to more human-readable format.

The execution plan always has a format:

```
PLAN (plan_definition) ie PLAN (A ORDER IDX1
INDEX (IDX2, IDX3))
```

for example,

select * from STUDENT
where CODE = 'SK765'
PLAN (STUDENT NATURAL)

Further information on Firebird's optimizer and it's Plan can be found at the link below:

https://www.firebirdsql.org/en/news/understanding-the-firebird-optimizer-and-it-s-plans/

### *General rule of thumb tips...*

The following are by no means a definitive list but just a few helpful tips.

- Using LIKE is slow. Where possible use FULLTEXT over LIKE.
- Use derived tables to optimize SELECT with ORDER BY/GROUP BY.
- Never retrieve more data than you need. That is, avoid the SELECT * (wildcard).
- Use indexing in tables correctly.
- Using UNION over OR in your SELECT statement can significantly improve performance.
- Routinely monitor your optimization plan. Along with table optimization.
- Perform Routine garbage collection management.
- There are many ways to write SELECT statements as we've seen. Experiment with JOIN, UNIONS, sub-queries, etc to find the optimum for your database.

In closing there is a great article on the internet called "*45 Ways To Speed Up Firebird Database*"
you can find it here: https://ib-aid.com/en/articles/45-ways-to-speed-up-firebird-database/

# 31  What to expect in Firebird 4.0

As of 13<sup>th</sup> February 2019 Firebird 4.0 is at Beta. However.

So what can we expect in version 4 particularly in regards to what you have learnt so far?

Well for starters:

### *Granting a Role to Another Role...*

Firebird 4 allows a role to be granted to another role (see chapter on introduction to roles) "—" a phenomenon that has been nicknamed "cumulative roles". If you hear that term, it is referring to roles that are embedded within other roles by way of GRANT ROLE a TO ROLE b, something Firebird would not allow before.

ⓘ Take careful note that the GRANT ROLE syntax has been extended, along with its effects.

Syntax

```
GRANT [DEFAULT] <role name> TO [USER | ROLE] <user/role name> [WITH
ADMIN OPTION];
REVOKE [DEFAULT] <role name> FROM [USER | ROLE] <user/role name>
[WITH ADMIN OPTION];
```

### *DDL Enhancements...*

Enhancements have been added to the SQL data definition language lexicon in Firebird 4 and include a new, high precision floating-point data type and more extensions for the IDENTITY type.

New and extended DDL statements supporting the new security features are also added.

### Data Manipulation Language (DML)...

Support has been implemented to enable the declared default value for a column or domain to be included directly in INSERT, UPDATE, MERGE and UPDATE OR INSERT statements by use of the keyword DEFAULT in the column's position. If DEFAULT appears in the position of a column that has no default value defined, the engine will attempt to write NULL to that column.

### Procedural SQL (PSQL)...

Recursion is now supported in sub-routines. A few improvements have been implemented to help in logging exceptions from the various error contexts supported in PSQL.

### Bug Fixes...

No system is perfect therefore we can expect a number of bug fixes to be addressed in version 4.

This is by no means an extensive list of enhancements and added features we can expect. For more in formation you can visit: https://www.firebirdsql.org/en/planning-board/

and for a more detailed description compiled by Helen Borrie visit: http://web.firebirdsql.org/downloads/prerelease/v40beta1/Firebird-4.0.0_Beta1-ReleaseNotes.pdf

# 32 Firebird in Action – LibreOffice Base Application

### *Getting started...*

Now that you have reached this far, it is time to impress your department head and build a Firebird database application! You can do it!

LibreOffice Base is part of LibreOffice's suite of productivity computer office tools. LibreOffice is available on platforms such as Linux, Windows and Mac. It usually comes as a default suite in most Linux distros. If it is not currently installed on your system, head on over to

https://www.libreoffice.org/

- then download and install the version suitable for your computer system.

LibreOffice comes ready to use with an embedded version of Firebird. But it is still in experimental mode and as such is not set as the default database.

To enable this feature select *Tools* from your menu bar, then select *options.*
Select Advanced and check *Enable experimental features (caution: some features may be unstable).*

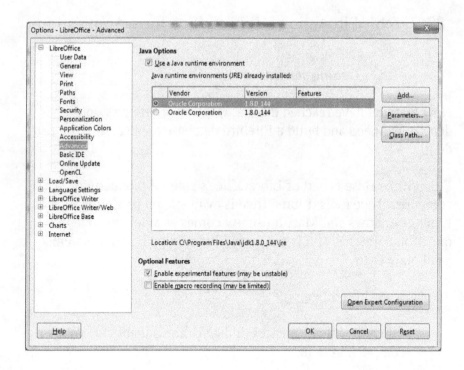

then Click ok.

This option will allow you to create a Firebird database.

Although we could use the term LibreOffice Base (I will refer to it
as simply LO Base from now on). We could if needs be connect to
our existing database via our ODBC dsn MyFirebird. However in
this case we will use the Firebird that is shipped with LO Base. This
will allow the user to see how to create tables in LO Base as well as
it's full integration.

We will be developing a simple Employee demographic information
database with a few forms, navigation, and a few tables. There will
be very little if any at all programming code. This is simply to
demonstrate the power and ease with which a novice or non-
programmer can implement a usable application, with the right tools
that are ready to hand and at zero cost. (Pause: "Who said there is

no such thing as a 'free' lunch?" A small but well rewarded effort is required on your part, with this getting started guide).

*Designing the tables...*

Three tables will be needed, these are:

- system configuration table to hold all configuration, drop-down options, any default parameters, etc.
- person table to hold all the contact details and
- sub-person table to hold such details as next of kin, emergency contacts, etc.

We begin by creating tblperson, tblsysconfig, and tblsubform.

Notice, for table objects we prefix the table names with 'tbl'. This is simply my personal preference. Some developers use the prefix 'tbl_, 'others simply omit the prefix alogether. I find readability easier, and therefore queries will be prefixed with qry, forms with frm, etc.

We will begin by creating our *tblsysconfig* table and follow by its data-entry form *frmsysconfig*.

Launch LO Base and select Firebird from the embedded database option:

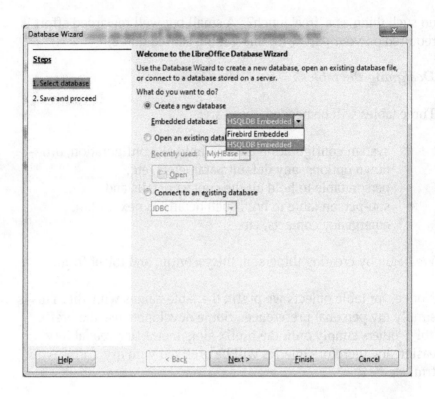

286

and select Next.

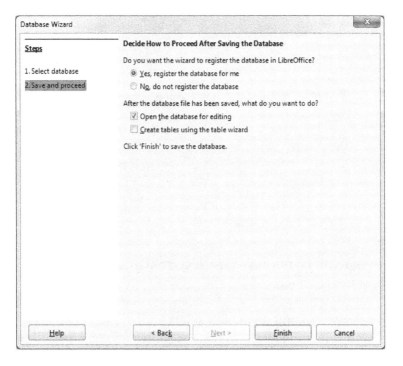

Ensure that 'Yes, register the database for me' is selected. This will make the database available to the entire LibreOffice Suit such as calc, writer, etc. Also ensure 'Open the database for editing' is checked.

Click Finish.

This will open a *save* screen dialog window. Name the file: *empContact.odb* and save it in the same folder as *MyApp.fdb* e.g. For windows users: *C:\myapp\data*. You should now be presented with the following screen:

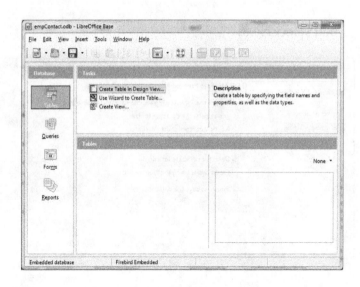

Our first task will be to create the *tblsysconfig* table and the data-entry form *frmsysconfig*.

Under Database column on the left select *Tables* and under Task select *Create Table in Design View…* as shown above, you will be presented with the following screen:

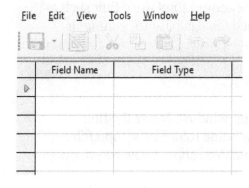

Enter the first Field Name as id and Field Type as Integer and set Auto Number to Yes As shown below:

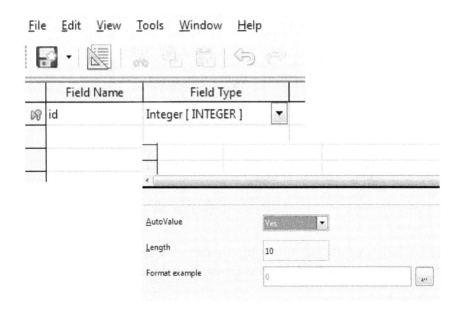

Populate the rest as follows:

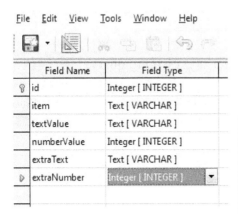

Make all Text fields Length 250.

Once completed click the save button and name table tbtsysconfig as shown below.

Notice that LO Base allows the user to graphically create tables. Now, being a pro you will know exactly what is happening in the background when the *Save As* [OK] button is clicked.

Select *File* and *Close* to close the Table design view.

Also notice the little yellow key next to id field:

| Field Na |
|---|
| 🔑 id |

This represents the primary key.

Now we have our *tblsysconfig* table we can now create our *frmsysconfig* form(s). This form will also contain a subform.

### Working with forms...

Although we could have our form directly bound to our table, this is not the preferred practice. Forms tend to be bound to an underlying query that is based on the table. By doing so we can use the query as filter by passing it parameters if required.

Therefore we need to first create our *qrysysconfig* query.

From the main LO Base screen now select *Queries* and then select *Create Query in Design View...*

Click the *Add* button as shown below:

Then close the Add Table or Query panel, by clicking the close button.

You can either double click each field to populate the grid below or select each field from the grid.

Populate the grid as shown below:

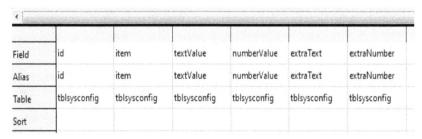

| Field | id | item | textValue | numberValue | extraText | extraNumber |
|-------|-----|------|-----------|-------------|-----------|-------------|
| Alias | id | item | textValue | numberValue | extraText | extraNumber |
| Table | tblsysconfig | tblsysconfig | tblsysconfig | tblsysconfig | tblsysconfig | tblsysconfig |
| Sort | | | | | | |

Click the *save* button and name the query *qrysysconfig*

Because our system configuration form will also have a subform we also need to create a subquery that our subform will be based on. Therefore repeat the above steps for *qrysysconfig* but give it the name **qrysysconfiglist**

We will be returning to our query shortly, but for now let us create our *frmsysconfig* form.

When creating forms this is where you can bring out that artistic flare inside you! However, to keep this book to a minimum, we will stick to a "straight vanilla, no bells or whistles" database look. Select *File* and *Close* to close the *Create Query in Design View...* screen.

### Creating a Data-Entry form with subform...

We will now create a Data-Entry form for entering system configuration data into our *tblsysconfig* table. This form will also consist of a subform. This time we will let LO Base do most of the heavy lifting by using the wizard.

Now, from the main LO Base screen select *Forms* and select *Use Wizard* to create *Form...*

Populate the form as shown below:

The main form will also contain our subform.

Now, from the main LO Base screen select *Forms* and select *Use Wizard* to create *Form...*

Populate as shown below and click Next:

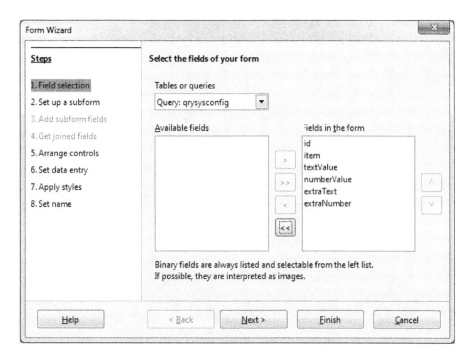

This time select Add Subform option as shown below:

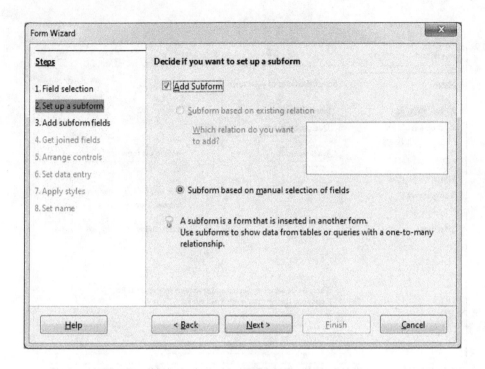

Now click *Next*.

Populate the following form as shown below:

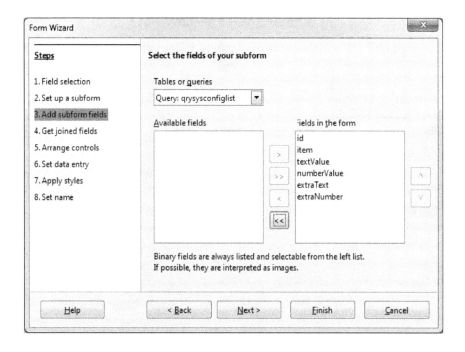

Now click *Next*.

Now populate the following form as shown below:

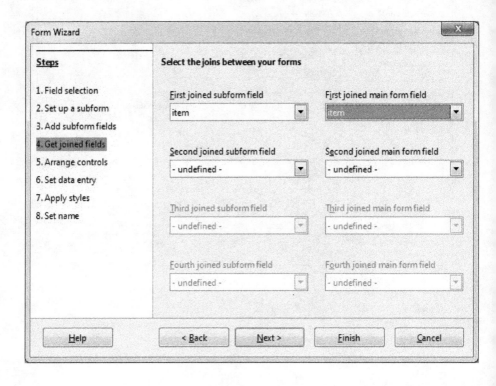

Now click *Next*.

Now select the main form arrangement as follows, then click *Next*.

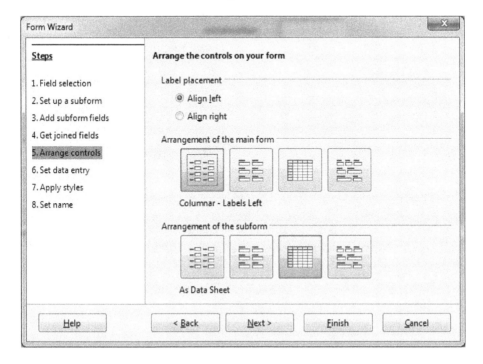

Click *Next* again to accept the Set data entry default option.

Select the following, and click *Next*.

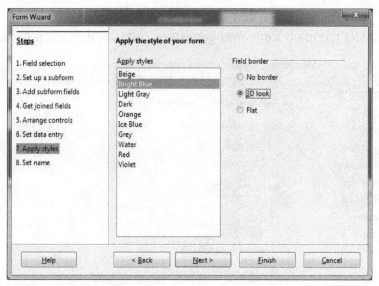

And set the Name to *frmsysconfig* and click *Finish*.

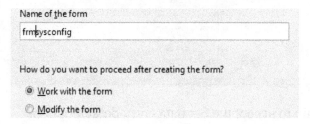

You should have the following Data-Entry form for storing our system configuration data.

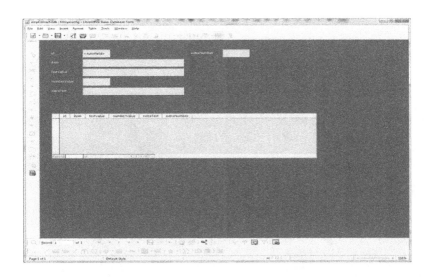

We can test this as follows:

In order for us to toggle between design mode and run mode class the form, once again, then right mouse-click on *frmsysconfig* and select *Edit*. The form will appear in design mode. Now at the bottom left click the design-mode toggle button.

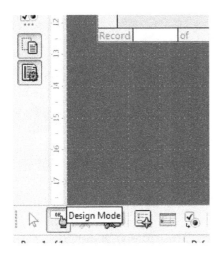

For our first data entry we will enter Gender type information: enter the following:

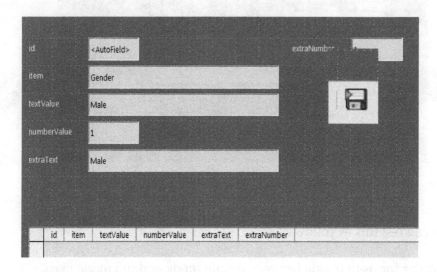

You should notice on saving our entry the information appears in the list.

Now to enter the next record you will need to click the *New Record* button.

Noticed that once you click the *New Record* button all your entries will be cleared. Not to worry. They are still in the database, remember the list is linked to items therefore no item will show no item list. Now enter item = Gender, textValue = Female, numberValue = 2, etraText = Male, extraNumber = 2.

And again click the *Save* button. This time you should see two entries in the list as follows:

| item | textValue | numberValue | extraText | extraNumber |
|---|---|---|---|---|
| Gender | Male | 1 | Male | 1 |
| Gender | Female | 2 | Female | 2 |

## *Navigating between the records...*

To scroll between records simply click the left and right navigation buttons as shown below:

## *Presentation matters...*

Now as it stands we could leave it here but I am sure you will agree that it could do with a little touch-up in presentation.

We need therefore to switch back to design mode. Click the *design mode.*

Our first change will be to change the labels description.

Changing textValue label:

On your keyboard hold the *Ctrl* and click the *textValue* label, this will hightlight the label as shown below:

Right mouse-click
and select Control...

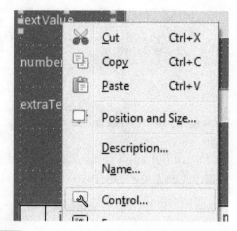

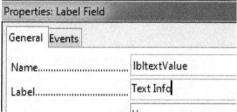

and edit the Label to read Text Info as shown here:

Repeat the process for the rest of the form to appear as follows:

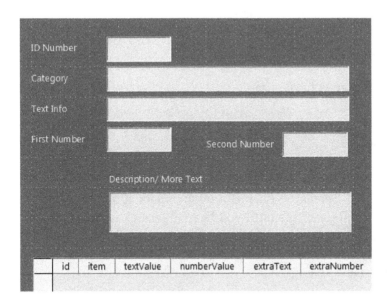

That looks much better. We can also simply edit the column heads. Simply Right mouse-click each column heading and select column…

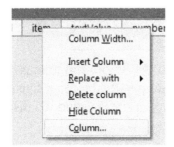

And edit each column as shown below:

| ID ... | Cat... | Text... | 1st No: | More Txt: | 2nd No: |
|--------|--------|---------|---------|-----------|---------|
|        |        |         |         |           |         |

## *Navigation Button (Roll Your Own)...*

Now that we have improved the look of our form, we now need to improve the feel. The navigation buttons are too small and does not feel that they are a part of the form.

Creating our own is fairly simple.

First we will place all the buttons on the form and position them where we wish.

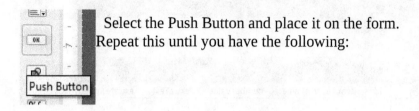 Select the Push Button and place it on the form. Repeat this until you have the following:

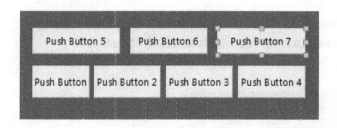

Next we will label each button. As before right mouse-click and select *Control...* This time also give the button a sensible name, for example, for a new record name it *btnNew* and it's display caption 'New'. As shown below:

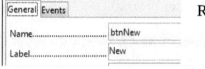 Repeat for the rest of the buttons:

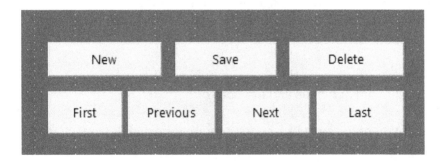

Optional: you could also enter Help text for each of your button. Scroll to the bottom of the properties window and enter some help text for example *New* could have a help text as New Record.

Now we will add our own navigational functionality to the form.

We will first add functionality to our New Record button.
Right mouse-click the New button the select *'control'* from the Properties Push Button window, under the General tab options, scroll down to Action and select from the list **New Record** as shown below:

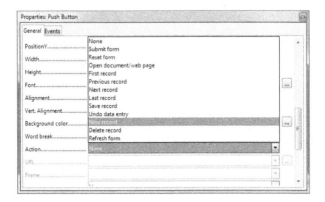

Repeat for the Save button select **Save record**, Delete Button select **Delete Record,** and so forth.

Once you have assigned an action to all the buttons, save your changes and change design mode to run mode by clicking the design-mode for run.

Now if everything is working, you should see the main form paging as you click the previous and next button.

Note, if you only see the List cursor moving up and down then you have assigned the button actions to the subform. This can be easily rectified. Select the Form Navigator button as shown below:

This will present you with the Form Navigator panel as shown here:

Form Navigator

Forms
MainForm
    SubForm
        SubForm_Grid
        btnFirst
        btnPrev
        btnNext
        btnLast
        btnNew
        btnSave
        btnDelete
    ABC  lblid
    fmtid
    ABC  lblitem
    txtitem
    ABC  lbltextValue
    txttextValue
    ABC  lblnumberValue
    fmtnumberValue
    ABC  lblextraText
    txtextraText
    ABC  lblextraNumber
    fmtextraNumber

Here you can see that the buttons are part of the subform tree view. To re-assign the buttons to be part of the MainForm simply Drag-n-Drop the buttons under the MainForm as shown below:

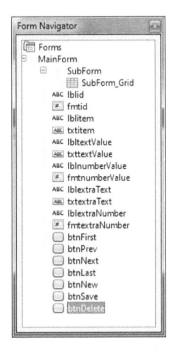

Now toggle back to run mode and re-test your form:

(remember to save your changes first)

Now all should be working fine.

As you can imagine there is a great deal that can be accomplished with LibreOffice Base.

Rather than focus on all the many features of LO Base if you are interested in developing Applications using Firebird Database with LibreOffice Front end, then I would recommend the following youTube link: https://www.youtube.com/watch?v=jWU0WdMJ2Kw

Here you will find a step-by-step tutorials on LO Base.

**d l y** *Things to try...*

1. Create a *tblperson* table.
2. Create a data-entry form for your *tblperson* table based on your *qryperson* query.

# 33  Why Use Firebird – in closing?

Congratulations you have reached the end of the book, but just the start to becoming a competent DB Administrator. By now you should be able to  confidently answer the question *"why use Firebird". I hope so!*

But just in case, here is a short recap to that question:

- Millions of developers around the world still use Firebird, meaning there are possibly tens of million applications using Firebird.
- Its zero maintenance needs makes it <u>ideal</u> for non-skilled DB Administrators, so you can experiment confidently.
- It's small foot-print makes it the ideal candidate for embedded applications.
- Thousands of Independent Software Vendors (ISV), such as LibreOffice ship Firebird with the application.
- Firebird is included in all Linux repositories and distributions
- Firebird can run either in embedded mode of a fully fledged Enterprise Database solution.
- Firebird has 4 Architectures
    - SuperClassic - ideal for Virtualized environments.
    - Classic – Heavy duty architecture for multi-CPU servers with large memory and fast HDD.
    - Superserver – Ideal for ISV server application.
    - Embedded – Lightweight single user fully blown DBMS in a DLL. Easy to upgrade to higher architecture.
- It is truly free to download and use.
- It has a large, friendly and mature community and you can join them too.
- When it comes to scalability Firebird is amongst the leaders as all four architecture are able to scale from 1 MB to 64 TB database size, from a single user to 1000s for concurrent users,

from embedded DLL to multi-cores/ CPUs.
- Firebird is multi-platform capable of running on all windows platforms, Linux, HP-Unix, Mac OS, FreeBSD, even Raspberry Pi, and more.
- It has a wide array of development tools from Free Pascal and Lazarus, PHP for Firebird, Firebird.NET, JAVA (JayBird), FireRuby, JDBC, and much more.
- A long active projects with version 4.0 currently in Beta-testing mode as of February 2019.

This is by no means a complete list of benefits, but just a few notes on why you should consider Firebird for your next project. I believe that Firebird's track record guarantees it a long and vibrant life and contribution to how we organise Database management.

Now that you have seen what Firebird has to offer, I would recommend those wishing to further their knowledge with the view to becoming a Firebird DB Developer/Administrator to checkout Helen Borrie's book *"The Firebird Book, A reference for Database Developers"*.

# 34 What Next

Having reached the end of the book, you may want to further advance your learning. But how do you do this?

- Consult others books like Helen Borrie's book *"The Firebird Book, A reference for Database Developers"*.
- Frequently visit the Firebird Website: https://www.firebirdsql.org/
- Join the Firebird community and keep up-to-date.
- Visit tutorials on YouTube website.

# 35 Appendix

## *Reserved Words*

| | | | |
|---|---|---|---|
| *ADD* | DATE | JOIN | RETURNING_VALUES |
| ADMIN | DAY | LEADING | RETURNS |
| ALL | DEC | LEFT | REVOKE |
| ALTER | DECIMAL | LIKE | RIGHT |
| AND | DECLARE | LONG | ROLLBACK |
| ANY | DEFAULT | LOWER | ROW_COUNT |
| AS | DELETE | MAX | ROWS |
| AT | DISCONNECT | MAXIMUM_SEGMENT | SAVEPOINT |
| AVG | DISTINCT | MERGE | SECOND |
| BEGIN | DOUBLE | MIN | SELECT |
| BETWEEN | DROP | MINUTE | SENSITIVE |
| BIGINT | ELSE | MONTH | SET |
| BIT_LENGTH | END | NATIONAL | SIMILAR |
| BLOB | ESCAPE | NATURAL | SMALLINT |
| BOTH | EXECUTE | NCHAR | SOME |
| BY | EXISTS | NO | SQLCODE |
| CASE | EXTERNAL | NOT | SQLSTATE (2.5.1) |
| CAST | EXTRACT | NULL | START |
| CHAR | FETCH | NUMERIC | SUM |
| CHAR_LENGTH | FILTER | OCTET_LENGTH | TABLE |
| CHARACTER | FLOAT | OF | THEN |
| CHARACTER_LENGTH | FOR | ON | TIME |
| CHECK | FOREIGN | ONLY | TIMESTAMP |
| CLOSE | FROM | OPEN | TO |
| COLLATE | FULL | OR | TRAILING |
| COLUMN | FUNCTION | ORDER | TRIGGER |
| COMMIT | GDSCODE | OUTER | TRIM |
| CONNECT | GLOBAL | PARAMETER | UNION |
| CONSTRAINT | GRANT | PLAN | UNIQUE |
| COUNT | GROUP | POSITION | UPDATE |
| CREATE | HAVING | POST_EVENT | UPPER |
| CROSS | HOUR | PRECISION | USER |
| CURRENT | IN | PRIMARY | USING |
| CURRENT_CONNECTION | INDEX | PROCEDURE | VALUE |
| CURRENT_DATE | INNER | RDB$DB_KEY | VALUES |
| CURRENT_ROLE | INSENSITIVE | REAL | VARCHAR |
| CURRENT_TIME | INSERT | RECORD_VERSION | VARIABLE |
| CURRENT_TIMESTAMP | INT | RECREATE | VARYING |
| CURRENT_TRANSACTION | INTEGER | RECURSIVE | VIEW |
| CURRENT_USER | INTO | REFERENCES | WHEN |
| CURSOR | IS | RELEASE | WHERE |
| | | | WHILE |
| | | | WITH |
| | | | YEAR |

# Other books by the same author.

Lazarus programming is a fascinating way to enjoy computing at all levels. Instead of simply running off-the-shelf, ready-made applications, you can free your mind to be the creator of your own work, using Lazarus.

Lazarus enables you to write your application for any platform. Lazarus with Free Pascal strives for: 'write once, compile anywhere'.

I hope that you get as excited about Lazarus as I have been in writing this book for you. If you are someone new to the software programming world, I am assuming that you have no prior knowledge of Lazarus and Free Pascal. However, I do assume that you have access to a PC and that you can install Lazarus with Free Pascal. I assume also, that you have internet access which will enable you to download and install the programs onto your PC. If you are someone coming from a different programming language, you can get up to speed with Lazarus quickly using this book.

Lazarus can be downloaded by going to the official Lazarus website, and following the links.

Throughout the book the term Lazarus is used to mean 'Lazarus with Free Pascal'. Lazarus is an Object-Oriented language. This book will get you familiar and up & running quickly with the world of Object-Oriented programming using Lazarus.

[x] Beginners          [x] Intermediate          [ ] Advanced

315